CONCILIUM

concilium   1991/3

AGING

Edited by

Lisa Sowle Cahill and
Dietmar Mieth

SCM Press · London

Trinity Press International · Philadelphia

June 1991

ISBN: 0 334 03008 0
ISSN 0010–5236

Typeset at The Spartan Press Ltd, Lymington, Hants
Printed by Dotesios Ltd, Trowbridge, Wilts

Concilium: Published February, April, June, August, October, December.

For the best and promptest service, new subscribers should apply as follows:
    US and Canadian subscribers:
Trinity Press International, 3725 Chestnut Street, Philadephia PA 19104
Fax: 215–387–8805
    UK and other subscribers:
SCM Press, 26–30 Tottenham Road, London N1 4BZ
Fax: 071–240 3776

Existing subscribers should direct any queries about their subscriptions as above.

Subscription rates are as follows:
United States and Canada: US $59.95
United Kingdom, Europe, the rest of the world (surface): £34.95
Airmail to countries outside Europe: £44.95

Further copies of this issue and copies of most back issues of *Concilium* are available at US $12.95 (US and Canada)/£6.95 rest of the world.

Contents

Editorial

It is simplistic to speak of old age in the singular and considerably more accurate to speak of it in the plural – to speak of the many ways and stages of growing old, in the world's many cultures. The meaning of age and its phases varies widely with factors such as class, gender, family structure, employment opportunities, retirement opportunities, and available health care. Yet, although every society of the world includes elderly members, the twentieth-century goal of the medical conquest of malnutrition and disease has effected the creation of a newly enlarged class of elderly persons, especially in Western societies. Various demographic, medical and economic factors have converged to create an elderly population which is twenty to twenty-five per cent of the total population of industrialized countries, replacing the small number of isolated individuals previously easier to assimilate in a younger population. Many older persons will confront an extensive period of retirement (withdrawal from economically productive labour before the onset of disability), lasting for fifteen to twenty, and occasionally even for twenty-five to thirty, years. Many more live for decades within a process of physical decline which poses for them questions of social contribution and dependency, as well as the confrontation with their own mortality. While it is still far too early to foresee the global consequences of a prolonged aging process, it is likely that the elderly population in the developing nations will also continue to grow and to pose cultural questions as serious as those now confronted by the industrialized nations.

The aging process presents not only medical and social questions, but also religious and spiritual ones. The elderly are not only a problem, a responsibility, or a resource for 'the younger generation'; to age is a task and a challenge for each one of us personally, as we grow older ourselves, listen emphatically to the experience of those who are going before, and enter the final stages of our own lives. Present Western approaches for confronting problems related to aging are limited and inadequate. An often untapped resource in the quest to deal with 'the problem of aging' is the insight of elderly persons themselves who reflect on their orientation and sense of meaning. Several authors in this volume make reference to their own engagement with the aging process and share wisdom about the intrinsic value and the moral and spiritual potential of that process. Moreover, non-Western cultures have much to teach the so-called 'developed' nations about the value of a long life and about the social integration of elders.

The first part of this issue will attempt to describe selected aspects of the phenomenon of aging as well as to broaden awareness of its dimensions. The second part will present theological, spiritual and pastoral reflections on aging. A third section will introduce some cross-cultural voices into the discussion. Although we make no pretensions to offer definitive conclusions on aging, we hope that a specifically ethical perspective will inform the issue: the evaluation of the goals, meaning, value and social consequences of human action and of social institutions, in an international forum. How can human communities recognize both the problems and the intrinsic value of old age, and shape institutions such as the family, employment and health care in ways that enhance the significance of the lives of elderly persons, and integrate them successfully into society and church? What does a specifically Christian perspective have to offer on these questions? While aging is clearly an ethical concern, it is also undeniably a concern of other areas represented in *Concilium*: pastoral and practical theology, spirituality, feminist theology, Third World and liberation theology. These other theological dimensions will complement the ethical in our quest for a more integral Christian understanding of the human aging process.

The first section of this volume describes aging and sets it in its social context. Rosa Fernández Herranz provides a physician's view of aging, not limited to biomedical data, but sensitive to the relational aspects of medical interactions with the aged and their families. She illustrates that it is not always easy to define the borderline between 'normal' and 'pathological' consequences of age. In any case, the physical degeneration which age represents inevitably carries repercussions for the most intimate identity of the self. The aged require a team approach to therapy in order to enable them to function most effectively in their environment. Gerardo Hernández Rodríguez substantiates the quantitative increase of the elderly population in industrialized countries in the present century and also differentiates demographically between women and men. The former are not only more numerous, but are more likely to spend their declining years in the single or widowed state. Elisabeth van der Lieth, including herself among three case studies of older women, explores issues of widowhood, dependency and health in Western society. She also raises questions about the agenda of medical 'progress' in defining the cultural response to aging and the accompanying decline of physical well-being. Daniel Callahan develops an analysis of the special problems which the availability of technology poses in health care for the elderly in industrialized nations, and questions attempts to extend the life span indefinitely, even when quality of life is vastly impaired. Callahan urges readers to balance 'curative' with 'caring' medicine, and to incorporate the health needs of other age-groups and additional social goods (education and housing) as considerations relevant to social policy decisions about medical care for the elderly.

The second part of this issue provides explicitly theological interpretations of the meaning of the aging process and of old age itself. Robert Martin-Achard demonstrates that the Hebrew Bible, without avoiding the burdens that old age can also bring, especially sees long life as God's gift and reward. The commandment to honour one's parents, while susceptible of many interpretations, today implies a responsibility to protect and succour the old. Christians are reminded that God brought forth the people Israel from an elderly couple without children, without hope, and seemingly without future. From a personal experiential foundation, Lady Oppenheimer confronts the almost universal human fear of old age; explores the interrelated aspects of old age as fruition, as decay, and as continuity in changing circumstances; and concludes that, for the Christian, old age can epitomize the mandate to 'live in the end time'. The task for the elderly is progressively to let go of all one's possessions.

Paul Schotsmans investigates the manner in which human beings can best realize their potential, and locates the total development of the elderly within this context. The grounding anthropological principles are the necessity of recognizing the uniqueness of each person, of having social relationships with God and others, and of participating in some form of community living in which personal independence is guaranteed. Eugene Bianchi (a layman), and Walter Burghardt, SJ (a priest), outline the prospects for a fruitful old age from two complementary directions: *action*, motivated by an altruism enhanced by one's life experiences and directed toward peace and justice (Bianchi); and *contemplation*, which arises from kenosis or 'self-emptying', and consists in 'a long loving look at the real' (Burghardt). Martina Blasberg-Kuhnke places the phenomenon of aging in the Christian community, as she argues not only that church ministry must reach out to the elderly, but also that the elderly can be a catalyst for the identity of the Christian community: a *koinonia* between young and old, who achieve solidarity in praxis.

A final section offering cross-cultural perspectives includes Asian,

African and Latin American representatives. These three illustrate the
greater importance of village and kinship networks in defining the place
and role of the elderly, while a fourth North American representative
attempts to recreate in a 'First World' context some of the structures
which have traditionally supported aged persons within the family. Mary
John Mananzan, OSB, contributes an overview of cultures in North
Asia, South Asia and Southeast Asia, showing how indigenous religious
systems have generally supported veneration of the elderly and their
wisdom; how Asian societies have included them in a sense of group
belonging; and how the present generation still maintains a high level of
respect for old people. At the same time, aged women and especially
widows can be quite disadvantaged, particularly if they have no sons to
care for them. Writing from Brazil, Ivone Gebara makes it clear that the
reverence for age which characterizes traditional societies must not be
romanticized, particularly when such cultures have been eroded and
exploited by the values and the economies of their rich neighbours. Old
people in the less developed nations, especially women, can also suffer
extreme burdens of poverty and be reduced to dependency, alienation
and marginalization. Under the influence of capitalist culture, these
nations, too, harbour a norm of productivity and an ideal of youth.
Gebara recommends a popular theology and ethics of old age in which
age is accepted as a part of one's own humanity, and in which to love and
serve the old would be to love and serve one's own future as well as God.
Bénézet Bujo emphasizes that in Africa elders are part of an integrated
and hierarchically ordered community which has its source in God. A
special function of the elderly is to enable the generation of today to live
out of the memory of previous generations. One of the tasks of African
culture is to preserve the history of past values, while moving into the
modern world.

Drew Christiansen, SJ, searches for a way to reinstitutionalize in the
'First World' the family-centred approach to aging still typical of Asia
and Africa. The ideals of the young are autonomy and freedom, but
other sources of human dignity are physical care and social cultivation –
continuing needs of the old best provided within the family. Christiansen urges social and financial supports for families engaged in 'eldercare'. A family-based model of care could not only meet the physical
demands of the elderly, but could also provide intergenerational friendship for older people who strive to integrate their lives, face up to loss,
and prepare for death.

The contributions to this issue of *Concilium* reflect the continuing
strong influence of European and North American cultures on Roman
Catholic theology and ethics. We hope nonetheless that these cultures

have been brought into productive dialogue with theological reflection and social analysis emerging from some of the world's other cultures and social realities.

Lisa Sowle Cahill
Dietmar Mieth

I · Aging and its Social Context

Bio-Medical Aspects of Aging

Rosa Fernández Herranz

Introduction

One of the most serious problems facing the developed world at present is undoubtedly the progressive aging of its population, with all the personal, family and social problems this entails.

The causes are partly the diminished birth-rate, and partly increased life-expectancy resulting from advances made in the fields of hygiene, nutrition and health care.

Aging, though, besides being a biological and social phenomenon, is first a human fact: it is persons, human beings, who age, who feel their own bodies' and minds' growing incapacity and progressive deterioration; who feel, too, their family circle, their economic situation, their work and social structure gradually coming apart around them.

The experience of aging and its repercussion on individuals' innermost being is going to depend basically on old people's physical and psychic state of health, on their approach to the fact of old age, and their family and social surroundings.

1. Features of physiological aging

Aging is a biological process, characterized by a series of somatic and psychic changes, which appear inexorably with the passage of time and deeply affect a person's life. These can be summarized as follows:

During the aging process, all functions of the organism (cardiac-circulatory and nervous systems, sight, etc.) are going to be affected in an irregular and asynchronous manner by this decline, though not all changes will affect everyone with the same intensity, nor will they have the same repercussions on everyone's quality of life.

Besides this, not everyone will age in the same way: there are old people who preserve their autonomy, mental lucidity and general quality of life to the end of their days. Others, owing to the presence of various diseases, family and social maladjustments, and especially brain disorders (arteriosclerosis, dementia, etc.), are going to age with a host of associated problems, which, besides affecting them as persons, will sometimes have dramatic repercussions on their family and social circles.

It is not easy, however, to define the frontier between physiological and pathological aging, between a normal and a senile old person. As the years pass, deterioration becomes increasingly evident, and it is difficult to quantify and evaluate the point in this decline when normal aging crosses over into senility.

During the normal or physiological aging process, functional changes take place which will affect the various organs of the body and their functioning, unevenly but progressively:

With the passage of years, muscular strength and mass, balance and motor agility are lost, so that walking and all movements generally become slower and clumsier.

The bones undergo a progressive loss of calcium, making them more fragile and increasing the risk of fractures, crumbling of the spine, etc.

The joints gradually waste away, leading to frequent forms of arthritis, which can often be incapacitating and painful.

Cardiac capacity diminishes, as does that of the respiratory system, so that old people tire more easily and succumb more quickly to situations involving effort or stress.

The digestive system undergoes changes that can condition diet: loss of teeth, slowing-down of the digestive tract, difficulty in absorbing certain foods, etc.

In the urinary system, alterations in the functioning of the bladder can provoke periods of incontinence or urine retention, often aggravated, in men, by prostate problems. These alterations can have a severe effect on old people, both in their social life and in their own self-esteem.

Visual acuity diminishes with age, as does hearing, both of which produce difficulties in social relationships.

Male and female genital systems also undergo modifications, though sexual activity can be prolonged to an advanced age, depending more on psychological than properly organic factors.

The vascular system will be deeply affected, not only by the aging process in itself, but basically by association with arteriosclerosis, a process that affects virtually all old people and is one of the main causes of death and disability.

In the brain, the centre of the nervous system and the axis of life, there is a moderate but progressive loss of neurones, with a major diminution of inter-neuronal connections and modification of the different neuro-transmitters. These changes seem to be what are responsible for the psychic and intellectual modifications that characterize the advanced stages of the aging process.

Aging does not necessarily involve deterioration or loss of intellectual faculties. But advancing years generally bring a loss of memory, particularly of recent events, a lessening of capacity to acquire fresh knowledge, and increased difficulty in adapting to change and new situations. Intellectual output diminishes, as does power of concentration.

From the psychological aspect, old people will often reflect, in their behaviour and their mental state, the personal and social changes to which they are subjected. Loss of family and friends, particularly of one's spouse, material losses, lessening of physical capabilities, isolation from family and society, together with lack of motivation and the normal difficulties old people experience in adapting to new situations, will often combine to produce depressive states (unhappiness, lethargy and inability to face up to life); paranoid states, showing mistrust and irritability; or states of anxiety, anguish and frustration.

2. Commoner pathological symptoms of the aging process

The normal aging process can be altered by the onset of more or less incapacitating and painful illnesses, usually chronic, which have an overall effect on old people's life, activity and state of mind, limiting their functions and worsening their quality of life.

The results of the latest survey carried out in ten European countries (Eurotop Medical Geriatric Investigation) show that arthritis, arterial hypertension and arteriosclerosis are the processes that most commonly affect old people.

Together with these, other processes such as degenerative or vascular diseases of the brain, cancer, respiratory diseases and the like, can produce severe degrees of incapacity, often requiring health care for which the family may not be prepared, with unavoidable periods of nursing-home care or hospitalization.

These and other problems can affect old people singly, but it is more usual for several of them to co-exist in the same person, thereby limiting the therapeutic/rehabilitation possibilities in dealing with the functional incapacity to which they give rise.

This pluripathology typical of old people often involves the need for polytherapy, that is, the need for various forms of medical care at once; these can have side-effects which often build up to produce still further problems.

Furthermore, an acute process (a common cold, a surgical operation . . .) can have severe repercussions on old people's unstable physiological equilibrium, owing to their organism's lowered capacity for reaction and adaptation.

While all these diseases can modify and alter old people's lives, dementia, caused by Alzheimer's disease, among other things, is undoubtedly one of the most dramatic processes.

Alzheimer's disease is characterized by an irreversible process producing in sufferers a progressive deterioration of all their intellectual functions, critical faculty and personality. The first symptoms are generally lapses of memory, lack of capacity for abstract thought or change of character. Gradually, disorientation in time and space takes over. Language slowly breaks down till it becomes incomprehensible. In the advanced stages, sufferers are incapable of dressing or feeding themselves. They fail to recognize their closest relatives and lose control over their sphincters. Sufferers can live with their brain in a vegetative state and apparently devoid of any human content till some other illness intervenes and mercifully puts an end to their life.

Alzheimer's dementia affects five per cent of people over sixty-five and twenty per cent of those over eighty. Given the progressive aging of the population, this disease, the cause of which is unknown and for which there is at present no treatment, threatens to reach epidemic proportions by the year 2000, with all the problems this will bring for individuals, families and society.

3. Assessment of geriatric patients

Dealing with illness in old age represents a challenge to the medical profession at every stage, since illness in old age differs in its presentation, evolution and prognosis from the same stages in mature adults, and diagnosis presents difficulties due to unspecific clinical data and the risk accompanying the application of specific diagnostic methods.

Furthermore, with geriatric patients, the expression of various evolutionary changes can be confused with those of other affects, and vice-versa: symptoms proper to old age, such as amnesia of recent events, may be the first showings of a serious disease such as Alzheimer's; a phase of psychomotor agitation or depression may be the first symptom of dementia.

Recognizing the difference between an illness that gives rise to a specific incapacity and incapacity resulting from normal physiological deterioration is essential in order to avoid nihilistic and mistaken therapeutic approaches, which can also delay the application of effective treatment. Yet again, illness in old people can have the result of producing overall functional deterioration. Therefore, besides specific attention to diagnosing and treating the particular illness, an overall assessment of the patient's functional state has to be made so as to rank therapeutic activities in due order.

To help in making such an assessment, scales have been developed which analyse and quantify various parameters: simple daily activities, mental function, affectivity, motor or sensory capacity, etc. An integral study of the old person concerned, carried out by a multi-professional team including a doctor, a psychologist, a social worker, etc., will enable us to draw up a rational and functional therapeutic plan, with its different aspects – medical, rehabilitational and social – taking account of the family, hospital and social resources available in the community.

The application of suitable programmes of motor, language and memory rehabilitation and social adaptation, or of programmes of activities in everyday life, can, given good collaboration on the part of the family and social circle, improve old people's functional capacity, and prevent the onset of further incapacity.

4. Preventive and therapeutic aspects

The aging process, while basically a biological, genetically programmed, phenomenon, can undoubtedly be influenced by a variety of factors: type of life, cultural level, various illnesses, etc.

Preparing for old age, both physically and psychologically, is a process that should be started years earlier, and one that requires constant cultivation of one's physical, intellectual, emotional and human potential, as well as specific preventive measures, such as the following:

A proper regime, avoiding too sedentary a life and the abuse of drugs such as alcohol and tobacco, as well as certain medications. One must insist on the benefits of physical exercise and of a healthy and balanced diet.

Adaptation of one's environment – temperature, furniture, etc. – so as to avoid falls and other accidents in the home.

Early detection of risk factors, with regular checks on blood pressure, cholesterol levels, blood sugar, eye pressure . . .

Early detection of illnesses, since in many cases treatment in the initial stages has a decisive influence on the prognosis of life-expectancy and functioning.

Carrying out periodic general health checks is not always practicable for economic and social reasons. However, on the primary health care level, it is essential to detect and monitor groups at risk where the incidence of a pathology is most foreseeable, in order to carry out a more selective follow-up and devote proportionately greater resources. Such sub-groups would include: patients with pluri-pathology, risk factors or major functional changes; those who live on their own; those recently widowed, old people on the lower socio-economic scales and those who for various reasons have had to move house often.

With regard to the therapeutic approach, in view of the frequent pluri-pathology in these patients, different treatments should be given in order of importance, in relation to the seriousness of the various problems, never forgetting the general care and preventive measures needed to prevent future illnesses.

Drug prescription should be on a personal level, avoiding as far as possible polytherapy, with its risk of interaction among different medications and the building-up of side effects. To this end, both family and patient should be kept carefully informed so as to avoid incorrect treatments as well as patients prescribing their own drugs or failing to look after themselves.

On the medical-health care level, it is vital to give respectful and personalized attention, through a proper doctor-patient-family relationship. This should be based on mutual respect, on sincerity, trust and affectivity. It should allow old people to be listened to unhurriedly, in a proper atmosphere of calm and relaxation, in which their personality, character, circumstances and wishes can be understood and respected. Within such a cordial and respectful relationship of trust, the doctor can assess and explain, person-to-person, the diagnostic and therapeutic decisions to be taken in the case of each patient, and can give as much information and advice as seems appropriate to his or her physical, psychological and mental state.

In such a humanized relationship, the doctor, conscious that life is a good to be respected, but not the supreme and absolute value, can more easily avoid both the therapeutic obsession with preserving life at all costs, and the therapeutic nihilism that suggests abandoning a patient faced with an incurable disease or the onset of senility.

Translated by Paul Burns

The Demography of Aging

Gerardo Hernández Rodriguez

1. Setting the scene

'As you see yourself, I saw myself; as you see me, you will see yourself.' We should perhaps make this reflection every time we work out a plan, carry out an action or devise a policy related to old age. Old age cannot be something alien to or distant from us, since for some it is a reality now and for the rest will be tomorrow. And this tomorrow can be very close if we bear the relativity of the time dimension in mind.

Here, our concern is with quantitative aspects of the social reality represented by aging and old age.

The increase in the aged population throughout the industrialized world is obvious. It is basically due to increased life expectancy and the decline in the indices of birth and death, both of which are involved in the process of demographic transition.

This increase does not, however, mean that we are living longer than people have ever lived before; it means that there are more people living to an advanced age. We must not confuse individual longevity with an aging population.

The term 'aging' applied to a population is used to denominate a specific sector of the demographic make up of a population, one characterized both by a high proportion of old people and by a significant increase in this proportion.

An aged population corresponds to a society with high levels of development, industrialized and predominantly urban, since aging of the population is a demographic process with specific characteristics, which has been applicable to the most developed societies since the beginning of this century.

This increase in the number of old people affects present means of production, dominant models of family life, features and dimensions of dwellings, the social services and economic planning. The requirements of

the new demographic configuration in all these spheres produce major
social, economic, geographical and political concerns for governments at
present, and will mount a particular challenge to those of the future.

2. The demographic structure of old age

In Europe, the old continent, where the aging of the population is most
pronounced, the percentage of those aged over sixty-five in the member
states of the Council of Europe is 12.7% of the total population.

Detail of the figures corresponding to total population, old people and
the share of the total population they represent, with differentiation by sex
and their respective percentage shares of the over sixty-fives, is given for
each country in Table 1.

Table 1

Aged population in member states of the Council of Europe

(Figures in 100,000s)

Nation	Total	Population over 65	%	men	%	women	%
Austria	7,575.7	1,113.9	14.7	388.0	34.8	726.0	65.2
Belgium	9,858.9	1,375.9	14.0	537.1	39.5	838.8	60.5
Cyprus	673.1	70.5	10.5	31.9	45.2	38.6	54.8
Denmark	5,129.3	791.0	15.4	327.6	41.4	463.4	58.6
France	55,754.0	7,568.0	13.6	2,939.1	38.8	4,628.9	61.2
Germany (W)	61,104.5	9,273.1	15.2	3,162.3	34.1	6,110.8	65.9
Greece	9,978.0	1,351.9	13.5	592.3	43.8	759.5	56.2
Iceland	247.5	26.0	10.5	11.6	44.4	14.5	55.6
Ireland	3,543.0	388.2	11.0	169.8	43.7	218.4	56.3
Italy	57,290.0	7,664.0	13.4	3,076.0	40.1	4,588.0	59.9
Liechtenstein	27.4	2.6	9.5	1.1	41.0	1.5	59.0
Luxembourg	369.5	49.2	13.3	18.6	37.8	30.6	62.2
Malta	345.6	34.7	10.0	15.0	43.2	19.7	56.8
Netherlands	14,615.1	1,804.0	12.3	721.9	40.0	1,082.0	60.0
Norway	4,175.5	670.1	16.0	280.0	41.8	390.2	58.2
Portugal	10,230.0	1,264.8	12.4	516.1	40.8	748.7	59.2
Spain	38,996.2	4,824.6	12.4	2,012.0	41.7	2,811.6	58.3
Sweden	8,414.0	1,493.0	17.7	637.0	42.7	854.0	57.3
Switzerland	6,566.8	946.7	14.4	378.3	40.0	568.4	60.0
Turkey	52,059.0	2,125.0	4.1	952.0	44.8	1,173.0	55.2
United Kingdom	56,768.3	8,682.5	15.3	3,427.1	39.5	5,255.4	60.5
Total	403,721.4	51,519.7	12.7	20,194.8	39.2	31,322.0	60.8

(Source: '*Recent Demographic Developments in the Member States of the Council of Europe*'
Strasbourg 1989)

The highest indices of aging are found in the most developed countries; so, for example, Sweden and the United Kingdom have a percentage of over sixty-fives of 17.7 and 15.3 respectively, while Turkey, with a birth rate of around 29 per 1000, has a 4.1% share of old people.

The causes of an aging population or a population with a high share of old people are not the same in all countries. In some cases (such as the Nordic countries: Denmark, Norway and Sweden) it is due to a drastic and voluntary reduction in births: in others, such as Germany (and independently of the fact that here too there has been a recent falling-off in the birth rate), there is also the effect of the Second World War, in which this country suffered a large number of deaths, and had a large number of its men in captivity, as prisoners of war, for a time, which, together with other factors related to the outcome of the war, limited and delayed the reproductive process. In countries with low indices of life expectancy, the aged population is smaller, as can be seen in the so-called Third World.

In any case, there has been a marked tendency to limit the birth rate in the most industrialized and developed countries over the last decades. This, together with the lower mortality rate, plus some of the causes adduced above, has given rise to the following relations between the number of persons over sixty-five and the number of those under fourteen: Germany (Federal Republic) 102.4%, Sweden 99.4%, Denmark 87.8%, Switzerland 84.4%, Norway 82.5% and the United Kingdom 80.4%. Compare these with countries where the numbers of those in the early years are far higher than those over sixty-five: Turkey, with 11.3 old people for every 100 under fourteen, Ireland with 38.3, and Cyprus, Iceland, Liechtenstein and Malta with percentages ranging between 40 and 48%.

3. Life expectancy

The index of median life-expectancy at birth has evolved spectacularly since the beginning of this century in the more developed countries. The figures bear the same relationship to one another as the current difference between life-expectancy in the developed and the less developed countries now.

Everywhere, however, the female sex enjoys greater life-expectancy. Iceland and Japan are currently the countries with the highest figures: 80.2 and 80.18 years respectively. They also have the highest figures for male life expectancy: 74.54 years in Japan and 73.96 in Iceland. In the 1970s, Sweden had the highest figures: 76.54 for women and 71.85 for men. The two countries now at the head of the league have experienced a considerable increase, since in 1965 the figures for Iceland were 76.2 for women and 70.8 for men, and in Japan in 1968, 74.3 and 69.05 respectively.

The countries with the lowest expectancy at birth have also varied since fifteen or twenty years ago. Then, the countries with the lowest life expectancy were Upper Volta, with thirty-one years for women and thirty-two for men in 1961, and Chad, with thirty-five for women and twenty-nine for men in 1964. In the 1980s, the least favourable figures were found in Sierra Leone and Gambia, with respective figures of 33.5 and 36.5 for women and 32.5 and 33.5 for men, both in 1985.

4. The demographic relation between the sexes

A feature common to all the statistical data relating to advanced age is the considerable quantitative supremacy of women over men.

In infancy, childhood and early youth, since more boys than girls are born and despite the fact that the death rate is higher among boys from an early age, the male population outnumbers the female. Once one gets to adulthood, however, and especially into old age, there are many more women than men, because of women's proven superior biological survival capability.

In the population aged over sixty-five in the member states of the Council of Europe, the overall proportion is 60.8% women to 39.2% men. The most acute difference is in Germany (Federal Republic), with 65.9% women and 34.1% men; the smallest difference is in Cyprus, with 54.8% women and 45.2% men.

In relation to civil status

Because of the complexity of the socio-cultural differences among various countries, with differing family structures in terms of usages, customs, beliefs and religions, there is no space in the confines of this article for a detailed study of the specific demographic data relating to different civil status. We therefore have to run the risk of presenting an incomplete picture of this demographic aspect of population.

In some countries with a strong Catholic religious tradition there is greater permanence in the married state; in others, where civil marriage has long been the norm, accompanied by divorce, the scene is one of a high percentage of divorced people or those in second marriages. Others again, where a high level of pluralism and tolerance is the norm, show large numbers of non-institutionalized unions. Finally, some countries have social and religious systems which allow polygamy and repudiation.

In general, in the European socio-cultural setting, in which several of these systems co-exist, there is a tendency for women to outnumber men considerably in old age, whether they are widows or single. This tendency is less marked in countries where divorce is well established: this is because – while there are still more women than men in this age group – where divorce is established, one man can confer the status of married and divorced on several women successively, by contrast with those countries where divorce is less frequent and there are therefore more women who remain single or widowed.

The numerical supremacy of women in old age in both widowhood and spinsterhood is partly due to women's superior biological capability for surviving. The certainty of this fact, with its corollary that there are more women than men in the population, also explains both the preponderance of widows over widowers, and of single women over single men – both despite the fact that, as we have seen, more boys are born than girls.

Clearly, since there are more women than men in the overall population, there will be more single women than single men. There is also, however, a high proportion of widows in relation to the number of married women over sixty-five. There are various reasons for this, some biological and others sociological. Let us look at some of these:

It is logical that there should be a higher proportion of men than women among married people over sixty-five since the fact that men tend to marry later than women (though less so among the younger generation) means that when the men reach sixty-five, their wives have still not reached this age.

There is a greater number of widows than widowers by virtue of women's superior biological capacity for surviving, which gives them greater life expectancy.

In some countries, there is also the fact that, at least until recently, women were excluded from a number of occupations, jobs and pursuits which were held to be reserved to men. Because these tend to be dangerous or harmful to health, women have not suffered their effects on morbidity and mortality rates.

Difference in age between husband and wife, once they both reach old age, even supposing that both die at the same age, means that the wife will survive her husband as a widow for the same number of years as separates them in age.

Finally, there is the very influential sociological and statistical fact of the confluence of family and societal conditionings that influences the behaviour of widowers and widows, making them behave differently in relation to second marriages. The fact that widowers have a greater propensity to contract further marriages than widows affects population censuses by lowering the recorded number of widowers and raising that of married men, since all those men who are widowed and remarry between two censuses will be recorded as married men rather than widowers in the second. The greater frequency with which widowers remarry compared to widows also contributes to there being fewer of the former than of the latter.

5. Future projections

The problem of an aging population is not one that affects the whole world, nor is it identical in all countries where it does appear. At the present time it is a feature of the Western world, and within that has particular characteristics for each country. If the birth rate continues to decline in these countries, then they will have an increasingly aging population.

The figures given in Table 2 illustrate this. It gives OECD estimates for

Table 2

Population aged sixty-five and over (1980–2050) as percentage of total population

Country	1980	1990	2000	2010	2020	2030	2040	2050
Australia	9.6	11.3	11.7	12.6	15.4	18.2	19.7	19.4
Austria	15.5	14.6	14.9	17.5	19.4	22.8	23.9	21.7
Belgium	14.4	14.2	14.7	15.9	17.7	20.8	21.9	20.8
Canada	9.5	11.4	12.8	14.6	18.6	22.4	22.5	21.3
Denmark	14.4	15.3	14.9	16.7	20.1	22.6	24.7	23.2
Finland	12.0	13.1	14.4	16.8	21.7	23.8	23.1	22.7
France	14.0	13.8	15.3	16.3	19.5	21.8	22.7	22.3
Germany	15.5	15.5	17.1	20.4	21.7	25.8	27.6	24.5
Greece	13.1	12.3	15.0	16.8	17.8	19.5	21.0	21.1
Iceland	9.9	10.3	10.8	11.1	14.3	18.1	20.1	21.1
Ireland	10.7	11.3	11.1	11.1	12.6	14.7	16.9	18.9
Italy	13.5	13.8	15.3	17.3	19.4	21.9	24.2	22.6
Japan	9.1	11.4	15.2	18.6	20.9	20.0	22.7	22.3
Luxembourg	13.5	14.6	16.7	18.1	20.2	22.4	22.0	20.3
Netherlands	11.5	12.7	13.5	15.1	18.9	23,0	24.8	22.6
New Zealand	9.7	10.8	11.1	12.0	15.3	19.4	21.9	21.3
Norway	14.8	16.2	15.2	15.1	18.2	20.7	22.8	21.9
Portugal	10.2	11.8	13.5	14.1	15.6	18.2	20.4	20.6
Sweden	16.3	17.7	16.6	17.5	20.8	21.7	22.5	21.4
Switzerland	13.8	14.8	16.7	20.5	24.4	27.3	28.3	26.3
Turkey	4.7	4.0	5.0	5.5	7.0	8.9	10.2	11.5
United Kingdom	14.9	15.1	14.5	14.6	16.2	19.2	20.4	28.7
USA	11.3	12.2	12.5	12.8	16.2	19.5	19.8	19.3
OECD	12.2	13.0	13.9	15.3	17.9	20.5	21.9	21.2

(OECD average: for 1980, actual figures; for 1990–2050, foreseeable increase)

percentages of population aged over sixty-five for various countries throughout the world over the next sixty years. The figures show that in some countries, those aged over sixty-five will come to form over a quarter of their total populations.

The increase foreseen is greater, the lower the present birth rate or proportion of young people. So, for example, in the case of a nation with a large proportion of young people, such as Turkey, where in 1980 those under fifteen were 39% of the total population of the country, there is an increase in the proportion of old people foreseen, but this will scarcely bring the figure up to the present level in countries such as Spain, Portugal or the USA.

In conclusion, faced with a demographic picture of aging population such as presented above, we are bound to say that, from a sociological viewpoint, it is essential to develop – and where necessary to create – a favourable affective attitude to old people. This will apply on the family level and on the societal level in all its aspects. It is, unavoidably, a task that belongs to the family, to government and to society: one that they cannot and must not avoid if we are to progress towards an old age – which will be ours – different from and better than that prevailing today.

Translated by Paul Burns

'. . . and another will gird you and carry you where you do not wish to go' (*John 21.18*)

Elisabeth von der Lieth

The universal fact of experience that – at least in our culture – more and more people are living longer and longer and that the average life-expectancy of women in particular is increasing conceals very different individual fortunes. This difference relates not so much to the visible symptoms of the process of aging as to the subjective experience of this process and its effect on the spiritual equilibrium of those concerned. Even if we now limit the theme to old women and their families, there is a wide range of experience. How a woman experiences her own aging depends on many factors: the way in which those around her, and in particular the family, deal with the process of aging naturally depends on the extent and tempo of manifestations of physical decline, the degree of material security, and the capacity to reconcile the need for independence with insight into the need for care from others as that becomes necessary. 'She was the beloved centre of our family,' we often read in obituaries. If that is not the pious lie of a falsely understood piety, then the conditions for the old woman and her family must have been ideal. But in reality these ideal conditions are to be found far less often than the obituaries suggest.

I shall go on to describe three instances relating to the aging of women and their families. In so doing I shall attempt to formulate the questions raised by my own involved observation and as far as they concern me personally. I have changed the names.

I

Anna Müller, who was born in 1906, has been a widow since 1973. She lived, as she still does, in her daughter's house, in an apartment of her own, but is increasingly becoming integrated into her daughter's household, as her physical and mental powers rapidly decline. Until she was about seventy she not only kept her own home in spotless order, but also relieved her daughter of many household burdens, including looking after the children, making it possible for the daughter to go out and work as a teacher. Now she is no longer capable of doing even the simplest housework. A series of strokes over the course of several years landed her several times in hospital. Each time, after a short stay, she improved and could be discharged, but the improvement was only to her physical disabilities. Diminishing brain activity could not be reactivated. At an early stage her short-term memory failed dramatically, and later she also had difficulties in orientation. She was always anxious, and did not like to be left alone; as darkness fell she would close all the curtains and was only settled when all the members of the family were at home. As her mental capacities declined, so this anxiety increased, to the point that she could not be left for long even during the day. Although she was abundantly provided with all that she needed, in unguarded moments she plundered her daughter's refrigerator and hid her booty. The daughter realized that her mother was not responsible for this behaviour, but she still suffered as a result of her mother's 'moral' failings. There was never any question of the mother going into an old people's home. She could not have coped mentally with such a change, and the daughter would not have the heart for it. Slight relief has now been provided for the daughter by a home help sent by the local welfare service, who washes and dresses the mother, tends the sores on her legs and gives her medicine for the day. But the daughter, and of course her family, has to see to everything else. The feeling that things cannot get any better, but only worse, is a heavy burden on all of them. The daughter is tormented with guilt feelings, since she has not forgotten how much she owes to her mother. The whole family bears the burden patiently, but there is no question that here death would be a release for more than the old woman.

II

Maria Meier, born in 1912, is a war widow. Her husband was killed in an air raid while on leave at home, but she and her two-year-old son survived. She bravely took charge of her own life, finished her professional training and taught languages in a secondary school. Although she was of course very attached to her son, she did not cling to him anxiously and when one day he left to get married, she took things without any obvious difficulty. She liked her daughter-in-law, and soon became friends with her parents. But she kept her own home, became involved in the community, went on to learn Italian in her retirement, and her warm hospitality was prized by all. It became clear to her friends that she was aging when she spoke more slowly and in a rambling way, readily and often, but not in a very structured manner, and lived more in the past than in the future. She still travelled as before, but became increasingly nervous as she prepared for her journeys, and the small hitches piled up. In the end there was no disguising the fact that here a process of senility had set in relatively early, which began to damage her mental functions long before her body deteriorated.

That happened shortly after her seventy-seventh birthday. Maria Meier fell down in her bath during the night, and had to lie there until morning. In the hospital, the doctors diagnosed a fracture of the lumbar vertebrae. The patient's age and circulation made an operation impossible. For six weeks she lay on her back immobile, fed and looked after like a baby. After this time the fracture had healed, but her feet had become useless. After three months in a rehabilitation clinic the extremely painful therapy was successful to the point that Maria Meier can now stand again and walk a few hundred yards, but only in shapeless orthopaedic shoes and with the help of a Zimmer frame on wheels, on which she can support herself. In the clinic there was no investigation of her mental condition.

Maria Meier did not protest when her son found her a place in a church old people's home. It was clear to her that she could no longer look after herself, and so she did not complain about the loss of her independence. But despite the best possible outward surroundings, she is unhappy. Once a zealous reader, now she cannot cope with books; the record-player is unused and the new television does not interest her. However, she does telephone her son at the office several times a day, as she does her friend. She has nothing particular on her mind, but it is evident that she cannot cope or that she is tormented by anxieties which she cannot articulate. She does not have anything to do with the other people in the home, but wants her son to come every day if possible, and her friend too. The cheerful confidence in life which people all admired in her has given way to an intangible sorrow. She sees only the negative side of everything and one gets the impression that she does not really register the concern of her children, the loyalty of her friends who visit her regularly, or the affection of her grandchildren. She herself says that she is one of the privileged, but she suffers in an indeterminate yet very deep way over herself and her situation. Even the Bible study which is held in the home once a week does not bring her any consolation. The pastors come from outside and change too often; so far none of them has spoken to Maria Meier personally. Of course the whole thing could be called 'the depression of old age'. But that only identifies the suffering; it does not explain it and does not give it any meaning.

III

And now for myself. I was born in 1918, so I am now seventy-three and 'still' able to do a good deal. I am one of the older generation, but I can 'still' walk, swim, drive a car, look after my own home, entertain guests, fill in my tax forms, travel with grandchildren, and care for old people who are worse off than I am. So my existence swings between the 'still' of my own case and the 'no longer' of other old people and prompts reflections about how things will be when the 'no longer' applies to me.

Of course in my case, too, there is a 'no longer'. Whatever I do takes longer than it used to; I find it more arduous, and some things no longer interest me as much. I can no longer read or write for hours on end without my concentration flagging. In dealing with any audio-visual apparatus I am easily beaten by my ten-year-old grandson, and in the memory game by my seven-year-old granddaughter. I note the diminution in my powers with sorrow, but I struggle through to gratitude that so much has been left me. I do not feel that all the changes are only loss: patience, empathy, reflection can grow, and what happens to one can turn into reflected-on experiences. And sensitivity also grows. A disrespectful remark by my grandson goes deeper and has a more lasting effect than the renunciation of an activity which has become too strenuous.

IV

The proud assertion that average life-expectancy is increasing year by year in industrial societies must prompt suspicion. Before one uncritically hails medical progress, one must soberly consider the problems thrown up by old age – for the old people themselves and for their families. Here the material side is not the greatest factor in suffering, although a striking number of women who are now old need outside help. What is more important is the fact that in old age, difficulties increase which one has to get used to as long-term pains, and that freedom of movement is limited. However, in my view the decisive criterion for the suffering of old people is that in our society they no longer count for much, that their experiences and their advice are not sought, that the feeling of being useless is overwhelming, often long before mental powers in fact decline. Certainly there are great individual differences here, with astonishing exceptions where people remain physically and mentally sprightly until advanced old age; however, signs of decline are the rule, and they are all the more painful, the more vigorous, active and interesting life had been before-hand. For me the critical point at which I cease to praise 'progress' is the helplessness of many old people which makes them dependent. When the mother-child relationship is turned upside down and the occasional offering of help becomes total care; when one has to allow oneself to be looked after because one is no longer capable of deciding on even trivial everyday things; when one can no longer control bowels and bladder; when one can no longer look after one's own body, one becomes a permanent burden on those around because one is making undue demands on their strength and is restricting their free time. There are certainly instances in which nurses on whom such excessive demands are made still treat old patients respectfully, but that is not the rule. And how much dignity does that leave old people?

However, questions also arise in respect of the duties and rights of daughters or daughters-in-law. For as a rule these are the ones who have to bear the main burden of care for the elderly. Whereas sons and sons-in-law are praised and admired simply for tolerating their old mothers in the home, it seems to be taken for granted that daughters will invest time and strength in caring for them. This problem is intensified by the fact that in society as a whole the increasing number of old people, often in need of care, affects a middle generation in which for the first time in history women, too, increasingly are out at work, and a generation of women who are aware of themselves and find professional possibilities for advancement. As long as their own children are small and need their mothers, these mothers are also prepared to forego professional activity. But once the children have grown up, there should be a period when their mothers can shape their own lives. Many women have qualifications, want to work or to become involved in further education, travel, in short do all the things they have had to forego for a long time. And now an increasing number are confronted with the problem of old parents, especially old mothers.

For the generation which is now old, their own families are still the main point of reference. Many old women quite naturally cared for their old parents in their time, without feeling it a special burden. Three generations under a roof was the norm, above all in country areas. Of course there was also a generation problem then, but tensions were tolerated or resolved, and only rarely led to physical separation. Nowadays living conditions hardly allow a woman to grow old in the family. One may lament these changed family circumstances, but there is nothing one can do about them. Attempts are made with communities which embrace several generations and in which a shared task – for example running a farm – provides occupations for different ages and thus possibilities of integration. However, this calls for extraordinary conditions, and such an approach cannot be transferred to ordinary everyday life.

Now of course there are old people's homes, and nursing homes for the more severe cases. But good old people's homes, where the old people are looked after but not spoon-fed, cared for but not robbed of their independence, where they find stimulation and company, are expensive and within the reach of only a small number of people. For the majority of the old, the old people's home still represents a social come-down which involves loneliness, loss of independence and having to fit in with a more or less rigorous regime. All this applies to an even greater degree to nursing homes. The call for more and better homes, more and better-trained nurses, can be heard loud on all sides, but so too can the question where the money is to come from. Then suddenly the call for more family care of the elderly enters public discussion, and 'sending them' into a home is soon branded as lacking in love, with no concern to investigate the reasons for such a move or even to ask what the old people themselves want.

V

The constantly rising life-expectancy, especially of women, in our society is essentially the achievement of medical science, which in the meantime has in fact developed a special branch of geriatrics. Its aim is not just of course the simple prolongation of life, but the improvement of the quality of life for old people. But the present state of research shows that all human organs have been researched better and therefore can have more successful therapy than the brain, on the function of which so much nevertheless depends for human life in the full sense of the word. Operating technique has made a great deal of progress, and anaesthetics works with increasingly subtle means, and so it is increasingly possible to restore to life elderly patients who ten years ago could not have been saved. But the life to which the elderly patient is restored is often a damaged one, and the multiplicity of pharmaceutical products used for therapy cannot disguise the fact that true improvement is no longer possible.

After her last stroke (the eighth!) Anna Müller has been treated in hospital with a new combination of drugs. Every morning the geriatric nurse gives her an injection of seven drugs for the supply of blood to the brain, the activity of the heart and the dehydration of the body. Yet another dose is prepared for the evening. The old woman reluctantly lets this happen. If she did not have this injection, her heart would soon fail. Of course neither the nurse nor the daughter thinks in these terms. But the daughter would probably have been relieved if the doctors had let her mother die quietly in hospital.

Things are different with Maria Meier. She can still do many things that Anna Müller cannot. But in her case, too, her total passivity, her delivery over to an existence which is largely felt to be joyless, shows a deficiency for which medicine has no remedy. Perhaps she could be helped by more intensive and personal spiritual care, but the church home which is otherwise run so immaculately fails precisely at this point.

I have deliberately chosen examples which come from ordinary middle-class life, where neither lack of money nor lack of interest on the part of the children make life particularly difficult for old people. But precisely because these cases are so normal, they prompt reflection about what our future attitudes should be. And here theology, too, should put in a word.

One of the best traditions of the church is that for centuries it looked after the poor and sick, the old and handicapped, and in so doing became a model for the modern welfare state. But nowadays church old people's homes and nursing homes, too, suffer from the same lack of staff as state institutions, and they too can essentially do little more than follow medical instructions and provide the necessary nursing care. And that is not enough if one is to grow old with human dignity.

Of course I can see the whole problem in less than its ultimate sharpness because through faith in God's love I humbly accept even the most incomprehensible suffering of old age and trust that God will give meaning to damaged life even where we can no longer see any meaning in it. Yet the question will not go away, whether theology must not again ask what human life and human dignity are. Is there not too hasty and sometimes also too thoughtless talk about 'surrendering to God's holy will', addressed not least to the elderly who suffer both because of their lives and because of their families, almost collapsing under the burden of caring for the old? Is not what medical science calls its 'progress' too thoughtlessly confused with God's holy will? Theology should not produce any arguments for euthanasia – we Germans in particular have every reason to be extremely sensitive here. But a theological anthropology could perhaps make a science which has all too much faith in progress aware that the old catechism definition, 'man has understanding and free will', has not been abrogated, even if today new interpretations are certainly possible and necessary.

Translated by John Bowden

Ethics, Aging and Technology

Daniel Callahan

Human beings have always aged, become sick and died. Yet as long as life expectancies were short, and the course of illness brief, that biological reality posed no special problems. People died across the life cycle, with death as likely to the young as to the old. That situation has drastically changed. Health care for the elderly is bound to be the most serious long-term problem for the developed countries of the world. With an increased ratio of old to young (with the elderly the fastest-growing proportion of the population in many countries), and with over seventy-five per cent of most populations dying beyond the age of sixty-five, it can truly be said that the future of health care belongs to the elderly.

Some acute moral dilemmas arise because of this development. One of them is not so new, but is now intensified: should age be allowed to make a difference in decisions about patient care? That has certainly been the practice in most places, even if it is not openly defended or justified. Increasingly, however, the trend has been towards disallowing age as a standard for individual care. It is the individual medical need of the patient that is thought most morally relevant, not the age of the patient.

However, this development, with its rejection of a once-customary age discrimination, has been overshadowed by a still more serious problem. In the face of growing medical costs and scarcity of resources, will it either be possible or make good moral sense to provide health care for the elderly on an age-blind basis? The difficulty with a positive answer to that question is that it would then seem to entail an open-ended commitment to whatever technologies and whatever costs future medical advances may bring. If that is allowed to happen, then it is quite possible that the typically heavy demands for health care that are part of aging will begin to encroach on the needs of other age groups, or needs other than health in the society.

Limits to 'progress'

The deepest issue here is not aging as such, but the combination of an aging population and constant technological progress. There are just more and more ways of keeping elderly people alive at a higher and higher cost: dialysis, open heart surgery, artificial hips and various forms of intensive acute care treatment are already common with the elderly. Given the biological fact of aging, decline and human mortality, there are literally an infinite number of ways, actual and possible, to sustain aging bodies. The question, then, is this: how far do we want to go down the road of trying to combat death in the elderly and continue to extend the average human life span?

That question may be understand in two senses. One of them is to ask whether, quite apart from the costs, it is appropriate for medicine to seek to delay death in the elderly as long as possible. If we see death as a natural part of life, then we might be inclined to say that it ought, at some point, to be accepted as the biologically determined endpoint of aging. Yet we might well agree on that as a *general* proposition and still struggle hard to say just what that point should be. Death, we might say, should of course be accepted – but better next year than this year, and even better the year after that, and so on. We could, moreover, aim to have everyone live as long as biologically possible, say to 110, and invest heavily in research toward that end.

My own strong inclination, in response to those possibilities, is to say that we are under no special moral obligation to work indefinitely to extend the life of the elderly, or even to work to help everyone attain a maximum biological life span. It is not evident, for one thing, that adding years to life in and of itself increases happiness or spiritual development. Put another way, while death is always sad (not necessarily tragic), it is hard to see how one can see that there is great evil in death after a reasonably long life, even if this is not maximally long. Unless we are to count death at any age as 'premature', the death of an elderly person is part of life, not necessarily an offence to the value of life. Thus even if we had all the money in the world, and no other claims upon it, I am not persuaded that the spending of money continually to lengthen the life of the elderly would make much of a contribution to human welfare.

In any case, we do not have unlimited money available. Every developed nation is seeing powerful pressures on health-care costs, and beyond health care there are many other societal needs. One way or another, openly or in secret, we will have to set some boundaries on health care for the elderly. We cannot afford to press against all the biological frontiers of aging regardless of cost.

How are we to respond to this problem? We can, first of all, push to one side two responses that are attractive but inadequate. One of them is to say that a more efficient medicine, one less wasteful of resources and better grounded in assessment of technology, could help us provide the elderly with whatever care they need at an affordable price. But this is much too optimistic. No doubt a more efficient medicine could save more lives and bring better health at a lower cost than at present. But no degree of efficiency is likely to be able to cope with the high cost of life extension for the elderly in the future. Another is to say that if we would only spend more on research, we could find cures to those chronic and degenerative diseases that so devastatingly bring down the old. Yet there is no evidence that more research brings down costs; in fact it seems to increase them, mainly because the most difficult and expensive diseases of aging do not seem amenable to inexpensive immunization or public health approaches.

The great success of the biomedical sciences in all but eliminating the major infectious diseases should not lead to the conclusion that the degenerative diseases of aging will equally well be overcome. Cancer, heart disease, strokes and Alzheimer's disease are proving to be tough adversaries; no simple programme of prevention or immunization is likely to eliminate them. Even if that should miraculously happen, some other diseases would surely take their place.

All of this is simply to say that it is at least naive, and possibly irresponsible, to wager that the future will produce economic magic or stunning biomedical advances. We should, instead, work with the most likely future possibilities and develop our policies with them in mind. The most important historical trend has been towards (a) increasing life expectancy for the elderly, with a particularly great increase in those over the age of eighty-five, and (b) increased illness and disability accompanying that increase. Most importantly, we should assume for planning purposes that the increased success of acute care medicine in treating the elderly, especially prolonging their lives, will increase, as will the burden of morbidity. We are likely, then, to have more elderly people and more *sick* elderly people.

Three reforms are needed

How can we morally cope with that likely trend, especially if it would be a mistake to expect medical science to solve the problem for us? I believe that three great reforms in contemporary medicine will be needed, accompanied by some deep and underlying changes in our expectations.

The first change is to take seriously the idea that it may be neither morally necessary in itself, nor economically feasible, to continue working for medical progress of a kind designed to save and extend the life of the elderly.

We will increasingly have to ask what the long-term individual and social consequences of medical progress might be; the fact that a drug or procedure can save the life of an elderly person should not thereby establish its social acceptability. We will have to ask: 'What kind of life at what kind of cost?'

The second change will be to find a good balance between curative medicine and caring medicine. By the former I mean medicine orientated towards cure; by the latter medicine whose purpose is relief of suffering and psychological and social support. Contemporary biomedicine is powerfully biased towards cure, not care. Yet given the trend towards greater morbidity among the elderly, the great need in the future will be for care, not more cure. At the same time, a shift in the balance would also help to promote a better relationship between length of life and quality of life, a relationship ordinarily neglected in the enthusiasm for ever-changing curative medicine.

The third change may be to set some social limits on the extent of expensive curative medicine to be made available to the elderly, especially by setting limits on government benefits. This is of course a distasteful idea for many, and it is often argued that it would be a form of involuntary euthanasia. That is a wrong comparison. First, while there is surely a powerful moral obligation to provide decent health care for the elderly, it is hard to see how one could argue that the obligation is an unlimited one, which must follow every medical advance, however expensive. If there is an artificial heart developed some day, will we be as morally obligated to give it to someone aged one hundred as to someone aged forty, simply because it will save the life of the former as effectively as the life of the latter? Not in my opinion.

Second, the price of following medical progress wherever it might lead with the elderly would be to run the risk of serious injustice to the needs of other age-groups. Not only do the young have a powerful claim upon health care for obvious reasons; they can also be said to have a priority over the elderly in that they have not themselves become old. The elderly cannot claim an increased share of health care at the expense of those young people who themselves still need to live long enough to become old. Beyond the competing health needs of other age-groups there are additional societal needs as well. It would make little sense to weaken the educational system for the young, or tolerate a serious housing shortage for families, or allow cultural institutions to wither, in order to follow medical progress wherever it might lead with the elderly.

However painful it might seem to restrict health care for the elderly, I am here placing the emphasis on a limitation to the benefits of progress. If we could simply stop progress (which is not desirable in any case), we could almost certainly learn how to manage the health-care costs of aging societies. As an alternative to that, we will have to ration the progress. Is this so terrible? Not necessarily. The elderly in the developed societies of the world now live the longest lives in the history of the human race. There is little likelihood, given historical trends, that there will be a regression to shortened life-spans. A limit upon health care for the elderly would only slow down some forms of improved technological medicine. Limiting progress is not the same thing as limiting health care.

II · Christian Interpretations

Biblical Perspectives on Aging

'Abraham was old . . . and the Lord had blessed him' (*Gen. 24.1*)

Robert Martin-Achard

'Old is beautiful!' That could be the conclusion of careful readers of the Hebrew Bible (or Old Testament). They would note that Old Testament perspectives, like traditional 'Third World' views, are the opposite of a particular Western view of human existence which seeks to persuade us not only that nothing is more beautiful than youth, but that once youth is over, life is no longer worth living. 'Be young! Stay young!' is the message, repeated *ad nauseam*, of an advertising campaign aimed purely at making money, which the media perpetuate all day and every day.

The Hebrew Bible: Old age is God's gift

Certainly the Hebrew Bible, with the realism which characterizes it, does not ignore the infirmities associated with old age; it mentions the blindness of Isaac, who feels death approaching (Gen. 27.1ff.); the weariness of Moses, giving up further pursuit of his task (Deut. 31.1ff.); and the decrepitude of David, incapable of sorting out by himself the problem of his succession (I Kings 1). With the wise men of Egypt and elsewhere, the Hebrew Bible describes the decline of human faculties of a famous page: the evil days come which bring no pleasure, when the steps become uncertain and the voice quavering, 'because man goes to his eternal home, and the mourners already go about on the streets . . .' (Ecclesiastes 12.1–7). Barzillai is so old – eighty, in fact – that he no longer tastes what he eats or drinks (II Sam. 19.35 [Hebrew 36]), and the believer, coming to the end of his life, humbly asks his God to remain faithful to him despite his present decline: 'Do not cast me off in the time of old age; forsake me not when my strength is spent' (Ps. 71.9, 18; contrast 92.14 [Hebrew 13]).

Despite this clear insight into the miseries reserved for human beings at the end of their existence, the people of the old covenant generally thought that life was a good thing, the best of things, which makes all else possible, and that its prolongation was a manifest sign of the divine blessing.

The Israelites were profoundly attached to existence, so they wanted their days to be multiplied, in order that they could do all that they had to do. They did not aspire either to escape this world or to achieve immortality; they hoped to experience not eternity, but the full flourishing of their lives. They referred to the men of old, particularly the patriarchs who lived long lives and had a peaceful end; thus, according to Genesis, 'Abraham breathed his last and died in a good old age, an old man and full of years' (Gen. 25.8; cf. also 15.15; 35.29; 42.38, etc.). The terminology used in this connection does not suggest any resignation in face of the inexorable character of death, but satisfaction at a destiny taken to its conclusion: prolonged, fruitful and accomplished in peace.

The Hebrew Bible gives varied, not to say contradictory, indications of the length of human life. We shall not dwell here on the extraordinary figures mentioned in Genesis in connection with the antediluvian generations (for example in Gen. 5); some biblical passages seem to limit human life to 120 years (thus Gen. 6.3), a duration almost achieved by Joseph (Gen. 50.26) and Joshua (Josh. 24.29), who both died at the age of 110, according to a tradition which recalls information from Egypt. In a recent (1985) article, J.-P. Prevost is more reserved, basing himself on a statement in Ps. 90.10. He writes: 'If we are to believe the testimony of the psalmist . . . the sum of seventy years would represent a *maximal* hope (his italics) for life (a *terminus ad quem*), while eighty would be an achievement and an exception.' As for the idea of old age, which remains relative to its social and cultural context, the author notes two indications given by the Hebrew Bible itself. The average age of the kings who occupied the throne in Jerusalem from Amaziah to Hezekiah 'does not exceed forty-four years'; according to Num. 8.25f., 'at the age of fifty (the levite) left active service; he no longer worked': in other words, for the subordinate clergy in Jerusalem retirement age was around fifty. Prevost concludes that 'in all probability we can put old age between fifty and seventy' – an interesting remark, though a hypothetical one.

Israelite believers gave a positive welcome to life; they knew all the perspectives which it opened up, all the virtues that it offered. For them life was associated with light and happiness, with dignity and health, with abundance and piety. The ideal of the faithful is thus expressed in the description of the happy man who 'fears the Lord', as given in Ps. 128: he profits from the labours of his hands; he is surrounded by the numerous children whom his wife has given him; his days are prolonged; he shares in the prosperity of Jerusalem, the holy city. This is the vision of a countryman who likes simple and concrete facts which give his existence all its weight.

For the Hebrew Bible life is in fact inseparable from what we now call 'the quality of life'. There is no authentic existence such as God has willed for his human creation in pain and humiliation, in wretchedness and solitude, in sin and injustice. If Jeremiah (ch. 20) and Job (ch. 3) end up cursing the fact of being born, it is not life itself that they reject but its counterfeit, its caricature: the conditions imposed on them are intolerable; they cry out their distress and indignation to God. They feel that what they have been driven to is incompatible with the plan of the creator God and with the faithfulness which he has not ceased to show to his own.

Death already reigns, as the authors of the complaints gathered together in the book of Psalms (Pss. 6; 13; 22; 38; 51; 88; 130, etc.) put it so well, where the poor are trampled under, the sick set aside, the innocent condemned; where scorn, arrogance and baseness prevail . . . Here the old are particularly exposed to succumbing, while still alive, to the power of a destructive and maleficent force, the fearfulness and horror of which is denounced by the writings of the old covenant.

Nevertheless it remains true that life is and remains a gift of God: it is received from him and rediscovered in him; it is lived in communion with him. For Israel it is evident that only its bond with God assures the perpetuation of its life. Priests, prophets, legislators and wise men are united in reminding each generation of this and inviting them concretely to obey the divine will.

'Seek me and you will live', says Amos in the name of the God of Israel to a nation which is rushing to ruin, and he makes this more specific: 'Seek good and not evil, that you may live . . .', or again, 'establish justice in the gate' (Amos 5.4f., 6f., 14f.). Ezekiel echoes this two centuries later (Ezek. 18). Deuteronomy constantly returns to the fact that Israel can only continue to exist by observing the commandments of its God: 'Therefore you shall keep his statutes and his commandments, which I command you this day, that it may go well with you,' Moses solemnly proclaims, '. . . *that you may prolong your days* in the land which the Lord gives you . . .' (Deut. 4.40). This is matched by the last warning of the Deuteronomist preacher: 'I have set before you life and death, blessing and curse; therefore choose life, that you and your descendants may live, loving the Lord your God, obeying his voice, and cleaving to him. *For that means life to you and length of days* . . .' (Deut. 30.19). God takes the initiative – grace comes first – and snatches Israel out of slavery, makes it his people, gives it a land; now he asks it to respond to his love following the way that he marks out for it – then comes the Law to confirm the work of God. The divine prescriptions allow Israel to dwell in its land and see its days multiply (Deut. 5.33; 6.3, 18, 24; 10.13; 11.9; etc.). For their part, the wise men invite their disciples to follow their teaching; their maxims lead to life. 'If you want to live,' declares one master, 'keep my commandments' (Prov. 7.2); another proclaims: 'The fear of the Lord is a fountain of life, that one may avoid the snares of death' (Prov. 14.27). Wisdom herself speaks, inviting her pupils to join her: 'My son, do not forget my teaching . . . for length of days and years of life and abundant welfare will they give you' (Prov. 3.1). We might also recall this declaration: 'Hear, my son, and accept my words, that the years of your life may be many . . . Keep hold of instruction, do not let go; guard her, for she is your life' (Prov. 4.10, 13, 20f., etc.).

Honour your mother and your father

It is precisely this perspective which is attested in the fifth (or, according to another numbering, the fourth) commandment about honouring parents: *'Honour your father and your mother, that your days may be long in the land which the Lord your God gives you'* (Ex. 20.12); or, according to Deuteronomy, *'Honour your father and your mother, as the Lord your God has commanded you, that your days may be prolonged, and that it may go well with you, in the land which the Lord your God gives you'* (5.16). This apparently lucid statement raises questions on which specialists are far from agreeing. First, there is the problem of the original formulation of this commandment, which still remains. Recently (1982) F.-L. Hossfeld has sought to demonstrate the priority of Deut. 5.16 over Ex. 20.12, against the prevalent opinion; his argument drew an almost immediate response from A. Graupner (*Zeitschrift für die alttestamentliche Wissenschaft* 99, 1987, 318), and the discussion continues. The present text of both versions seems to have been the object of more or less extensive reworking: the promise, attached to the divine command ('that your days may be long . . .') is said to be secondary and Deuteronomistic in inspiration. According to some exegetes, the initial commandment will have consisted of the simple phrase 'Honour your father and mother' (R. Albertz, 1978), which is compared with a passage from the Holiness Code (H: Lev. 17–26): 'Everyone of you shall revere his mother and father' (Lev. 19.3a); in this connection note that v. 3 makes a close connection between reverence for ('fear' of) parents and observance of the sabbath (cf. the fourth and fifth commandments of the Decalogue), and above all that here the mother precedes the father, because she is the one who is more threatened (perhaps by widowhood).

Other comments have been made: thus H. Schmidt (1923) thought that this commandment had nothing to do with the primitive Decalogue meant for the people of Israel, since it was addressed only to children. However, that is to go too far. More interesting is the suggestion by certain biblical scholars (G. Beer already alluded to it in 1939 but rejected it) that the original divine directive could be reconstituted by giving it a negative formulation, like the majority of the commandments in the Decalogue. Taking as a basis texts like Ex. 21.17 and Lev. 20.9, something like this was suggested: 'You shall not dishonour either your father or your mother'. However, given the hypothetical character of this restoration, it is better for us to keep to the position defended by R. Albertz along with other specialists.

In his 1978 article, Albertz strikingly brought out the different 'types' of interpretation of the meaning of the fifth commandment, since here again commentators disagree over the intent of Ex. 20.12 and Deut. 5.16. A number of them, adopting a socio-phenomenological approach, connect the divine order expressed in these verses with the patriarchal organization of Israelite society. They stress the fact that, as in other cultures, the father and – in some spheres – also the mother enjoy undisputed authority; their honour is self-evident. The fifth commandment calls for an obedience which some do not hesitate to describe as absolute; ancient Israelite law even foresees that the child who strikes or insults one of its parents deserves death (Ex. 21.15, 17), and Deuteronomy envisages exemplary punishment for the rebellious son who imperils the social order by his obstinacy (Deut. 21.18–21). It has sometimes been thought that the formulation of the fifth commandment in the Decalogue is an attenuated form of original rules which were thought to be too rigorous. According to this interpretation, which puts the divine command in the context of *patria potestas*, it would be aimed above all at relations within the family: this was how the New Testament understood it (Eph. 6.1–4), though subsequently, in homiletical commentaries, it was extended to cover the authorities whom all believers must obey.

Another, more theological, reading of the commandment takes more note of its context; it recalls that the divine demand here is part of a complex, all of which must be taken into account. The fifth commandment follows a series of indications of what should be the attitude of Israel towards its God – it has even been supposed (as by H. Kremer, 1961) that it formed part of the 'first table' relating to God; it follows that parental authority is based on that of God, of whom the father and mother are representatives: it is only derivative. According to Kremer, parents are called to exercise the mission of preachers, teachers and priests among their descendants. This exegesis, some elements of which can also be found in Karl Barth, stresses the pedagogical role of parents; if it is sometimes challenged, it has the merit of bringing Ex. 20.12 and Deut. 5.16 out of their isolation and replacing them in the framework of the Decalogue and even of the history of the relations between God and his people. An ordinary sentence, with nothing original about it and which requires that children should honour their fathers and mothers, takes on particular emphasis when one knows the identity of the one who pronounces it (the God of Israel) and in what circumstances (the Sinai covenant, which follows the liberation of Israel)!

A third group of commentators opens up different perspectives: they do not defend the traditional idea that the fifth commandment is addressed to children, but are convinced that it relates to relationships between generations within the family. According to the biblical scholars who have argued for this exegesis for several decades, this takes up the immediate interests of the parents, relating to the life which children must care for even when the parents can no longer be of any use (Lev. 27.1–8). G. Beer in his 1939 commentary on Exodus already made the essential point: 'The Israelite must not treat harshly aged parents, those over sixty, whose capacity for work has diminished and whose life is valued less (Lev. 27.7); he has to give them their food and not drive them to emigration or suicide, far less kill them himself.'

R. Albertz also adopts this interpretation, which one can describe as sociological or even social: in his 1978 article he bases his demonstration on cuneiform legal evidence and Old Testament texts.

These three types of explanation are not necessarily mutually exclusive, and it is very probable that in the course of the centuries one or other reading has predominated over the others. It seems to me important today that we should note the relevance of the third interpretation.

'Honour your father and mother': the verb used in the Decalogue means 'respect another, give him or her their due, recognize their place within the community, with all the concrete implications that has'; the verb 'fear' read in Lev. 19.3 in practice has the same meaning. Old Testament warnings indicate that this commandment is not superfluous in the context of Israel. We have already noted the statements of the old Covenant Code in Ex. 21.15, 17: a son may not beat his father or mother and humiliate them (rather than 'curse', cf. also Deut. 27.16). The stress of wisdom on this point is revealing: 'He who does violence to his father and chases away his mother is a son who causes shame and brings reproach' says a maxim which indicates that he uses brutality towards one of his parents and expels the other from his home (Prov. 19.26); another maxim threatens: 'If one curses his father or his mother, his lamp will be put out in utter darkness' (Prov. 20.20); a third is perfectly clear about the attitude of some to their old parents: 'He who robs his father or his mother and says, "That is no transgression" is the companion of a man who destroys' (Prov. 28.24; cf. also 30.11, 17). Finally, there is the saying, 'Hearken to your father who begot you, and do not despise your mother when she is old' (Prov. 23.22;

contrast Prov. 1.8; 4.1ff.; 13.24, etc., and the long development in Sirach 3.1–16; Mal. 1.6, etc.).

In the light of passages in the Hebrew Bible which reveal the moral and social background of the people of God, the fifth commandment very opportunely reminds children who have become adults and fathers of the duties that they have towards their parents: this is a matter of looking after the whole of their lives and assuring them of food, clothing, lodging and even burial (Gen. 47.29ff.; Tobit 4.3ff.).

In old age: wisdom and hope

Here are two concluding remarks. As J.-P. Prevost invites us to do, we must distinguish old people from 'elders', though the same term, which originally denotes someone with a beard, is used for both. The former have seen their years multiply; they are recognizable by their white or grey hair, and they deserve to be honoured. 'You shall rise up before the hoary head, and honour the face of an old man, and you shall fear your God: I am the Lord,' we read in the Holiness Code (Lev. 19.32; cf. also Prov. 16.31; 20.29). Their great age has allowed them to acquire wisdom which is contested here and there (Ps. 119.100; Job 12.12; 32.4ff.). The latter, who contain within their ranks a certain number of mature, experienced and thus aged men, enjoy what is sometimes a crucial role in Israelite society: they form a kind of college, called on to take decisions which involve the existence of a people, above all before the inauguration of the monarchy and after its fall (Judg. 21.15ff.; I Sam. 8.4ff.; I Kings 12.6ff.; Ezra 5.5, 9; 6.7f., 14; Num. 11.16–30, etc.); Deuteronomy attributes to them a legal function of the first order (Deut. 19.11f.; 21.2ff., 18ff.; cf. also 22.13ff.; 25.7ff.), but not all the elders are old men and vice versa.

The Hebrew Bible sometimes gives us a portrait of people who have attained an advanced age. One thinks first of all of the patriarchs, whose destiny is related in Genesis, but also of Moses, remarkably fresh at the time of his death at the age of one hundred and twenty (Deut. 34.7; cf. Ps. 92.15f.; Ezek. 40.30f.), or of Job, full of good things and years after the terrible trial that he had to undergo (Job 42.10ff.). An anonymous prophet whose testimony has been collected in the book of Isaiah evokes the future status of Jerusalem in a world recreated by God, and the happiness of its inhabitants: 'No more shall there be in it an infant that lives but a few days, or an old man who does not fill out his days, for the child shall die a hundred years old . . .' (Isa. 65.16c–25). In the city destined for joy, while death has not completely disappeared, its time is so distant that it does not prevent God's guests from living in serenity and cheerfulness. The privilege of the patriarchs is as it were extended to all.

It is remarkable that the history of God with his people is inaugurated by an elderly couple, with no children, who from a human perspective have no hope of continuing their line through children and grandchildren. Genesis often stresses this point: Sarah is barren, and Abraham, full of years, can expect no future (Gen. 11.29f.; 15.3ff.; 16.2f.; 17.1ff., etc). Abraham and Sarah are going towards death, but their itinerary is met with a promise of life, life in superabundance (Gen. 12.1ff.; 13.14ff.; 15.5; 17.3ff., etc.); they bear witness in their great old age and until their deaths that their God is the God of the living (Gen. 23; 25; Mark 12.26f.). The Holy Scripture of Israel thus invites us to begin and end any study of our existences, which sometimes seem to be indefinitely prolonged, for a reason one does not know, in the light of the destiny of the patriarch and his wife which allowed our history to get under way.

Translated by John Bowden

Reflections on the Experience of Aging

Helen Oppenheimer

We all know that our lives are bounded by death and none of us can see beyond it. We have to look at human life as we may look at fish in an aquarium, from an underwater point of view, with the surface of the water overhead as a seemingly solid boundary. Believers may bear in mind that anybody up above could see what sort of pool we are placed in as well as watching us swimming about.

Unlike death, old age does not happen to everyone: but it may appear more real than death because people who have that experience can talk about it and we can see for ourselves what it looks like. Some people are more afraid of old age than of death; and some fear it as signifying the approach of death. Fears are better faced than pushed away: what is the best way to face the fear of old age?

Fear of aging

Christians may feel that fear should be altogether overcome by the gospel. This expectation can be unhelpful. To repeat 'Perfect love casts out fear' may only unhappily emphasize the imperfection of human love, paralysing people with inadequacy. As a way of understanding other people's dreads, ready-made answers can be extremely unhelpful; and when what one has dreaded begins to happen in one's own life, one can feel theoretical confidence melting away. It is more constructive to remember Gethsemane and not be too proud to be afraid. Far from being unworthy of a follower of Christ, fear may be one way of treading in the steps of the Lord. When the future is uncertain, the uncertainty itself can be a kind of cross.[1] What Christians ought to be saying to themselves and other people is not 'Fear is wrong' but 'When we are afraid, and especially when we are afraid of death, the Lord has been here first.' Fear must be met before it can be banished: it can be conquered in two stages, not in one move of dismissal.

Christians must stay in the gloomy or cheerful company of their fellow human beings. To be supernaturally insulated from either the major terrors or the minor anxieties of life is not part of the Christian hope. When old age is frightening, not as death's herald but for its own sake, Christians may feel as vulnerable as anyone. The Lord has not been here. He never took up this particular cross. He never had the experience of growing old: the consciousness of going downhill, the loss of powers, the outliving of usefulness, the expectation of being, at best, at the receiving end of benefits. Or rather, he did not have this experience drawn out through years, though surely his passion was all this in an accelerated form. His followers need not think of him as remote from what Teilhard de Chardin called the 'diminishments' of aging.[2] Christians who are growing old may still claim the encouragement suitable to an incarnational faith: no permission to opt directly out of human weakness and uncertainty, but something, or rather someone, to hold on to. It becomes Christians, like everyone else, to look squarely at whatever human life offers to alarm or content us.

Human life offers different things to different people. Is it even possible to say anything of general validity about the experience of aging? Until the experience is our own we cannot know whether to expect 'honour, love, obedience, troops of friends'[3] or 'second childishness and mere oblivion, Sans teeth, sans eyes, sans taste, sans everything'.[4] There are contrary images of aging jostling one another in our minds: old age as fruition; old age as decay; old age as no more than the latest stage of the journey for a person who feels like a twenty-year-old in disguise. How is one to steer between the stereotypes, reckoning with one's own experience but avoiding the assumption that it is the whole story?

Old age as fruition

If, being human, we need to make some use of stereotypes to give shape to our thinking, there is a lot to be said for adopting optimistic rather than pessimistic stereotypes. Expectations tend to be self-fulfilling. People who anticipate the worst duplicate their own troubles; people who have a habit of expecting the best are less often disappointed than one might fear. There is no need, in punctiliously avoiding wishful thinking, to go in for *un*wishful thinking. Here is a solid practical meaning of *faith*, characteristically founded on religious belief but with evident earthly as well as other worldly application. Faith and honesty ought not to be set against each other as a seductive voice whispering unreliable encouragement and a nagging voice whispering compulsory discouragement. Honesty provides the raw material. It tells us where we stand, or more often that we do not know exactly where we stand. Faith, or its real opposite scepticism, takes hold of the raw material and fashions it. To add year to year, birthday to birthday, is not *ex officio* loss or gain unless we make it one or the other. To think of human experience as a crop sown, nourished, watered and eventually gathered could suggest a more agricultural, less aggressive aspect, even for the dread figure of Death the Reaper.

Undoubtedly old age can be something to celebrate. Age can bring distinctive benefits: not to be presumptuously counted upon, often evidently a matter of good fortune not desert, but just as real and solid as the characteristic joys of youth. 'Thou shalt see thy children's children'[5] can be one of the best blessings ever pronounced upon a human being, and indeed it is not quick to come to fruition. To have 'old friends' takes time as well as friendliness. People who reach their golden weddings need the multiple good fortune of being married and of two people's reasonable longevity. Just to have learnt more, to have seen more and to have more experience to draw upon are benefits bestowed by time which even the brightest youngster will have to wait a while to attain. Does the French speaker who can say 'J'ai soixante-dix ans' have a better chance of accepting old age as a boon than the English speaker who has to say 'I *am* seventy'?

The image of age as fruition may be partial, but is not false. Old age can be, can characteristically be, a time for reaping a harvest, a time of maybe hard-won mellowness and serenity and developed experience truly called wisdom. Just because more of us now reach this stage of life, the hope of achieving the dignity as well as the span of time ought not to be held cheap, for other people or even for ourselves. Shakespeare's John of Gaunt could be called 'time-honoured'[6] at fifty-four: it takes maybe another thirty years to become venerable today. Must it be paradoxical to look forward to the maturity of age as a prize worth hoping for? People who have never thought in terms of accumulating wealth or glory can have something special to contribute by steadily accumulating time. A real live octogenarian is, so to say, charged with time, both as continuity and as change. Someone who is almost as old as this century can remember dressing in clothes familiar from old pictures, thinking thoughts which people today need imagination to understand, living through events which are now history.

'That is all very well,' the dear old lady may feel. 'What good is it to me to be a museum piece? It just means that I have had my life. I am a back number. What is so encouraging about that?' If that is what she feels, she can indeed stave off well-meant attempts to cheer her up, and lose the chance to be a conducting wire between the past and the future. But for anyone who values continuity in human life and the bonds which link the generations together, it could be encouraging and even inspiring to consider that one has the privilege of establishing the memories on which other people are going to build. The sort of faith that life is worth living which will be fit to stand up to vicissitudes is not readily founded on grand precepts but on maybe trivial details, of welcome and of hopefulness, bound together into a secure whole. 'My grandfather taught me how to do it.' 'And old friend of my mother's used to say, "A little help is worth a ton of sympathy".' 'When I smell box hedges I am back in their garden.' 'We could peer through the window and see the table laid.' 'She could remember being lifted up to wave to Queen Victoria.' 'They used to take us to the sweetshop and let us choose for ourselves.' Whether by fragments of reminiscence, by special little rituals or by unexpected informalities, it is in the capacity of the aged to give later generations lifelong memories. Provided that over-anxiousness, impatience and of course demanding presumption can somehow be kept at bay, even what may have seemed like boring duty at the time can be regarded in retrospect with affectionate nostalgia. In other words, when one is growing old it is not too late to take a long view of one's ability to make a difference to the world: encouragement admittedly more suited to the diffident than to people who have always had plenty of self-confidence.

The advance of old age can give a sort of everyday twist to the promise 'The meek shall inherit the earth'. To be offered a seat in a bus can be startling when one was still expecting to get up for one's seniors; but dare one admit how welcome this indulgence is? People who have sometimes experienced the scorn of their contemporaries for not being excellently agile and well co-ordinated may begin to enjoy the consideration of juniors who give a helping hand with tolerance or even respect rather than contempt. The tiredness which gradually makes itself felt if aging people try to do everything they have ever done turns out to carry no blame with it, unlike the deep, almost desperate, tiredness of young parents who reproach themselves for not enjoying every moment of their longed-for family lives.

The fragile self-confidence of youth is tempted to repudiate uncertainties and conceal ignorance. Maturity can be less anxious and take the more endearing motto, 'If you don't know, ask'. Life need not be like mountaineering, which gets more dangerous the further one gets. To look back over many years is less vertiginous than to look forward. We own the past in a way we can never own the future. Nobody can take the past away from us: it is not vulnerable to unsettling predictions that 'It won't last'. The serenity of age may not be a matter of other-worldly vision, but of a kind of stability. The stereotype of rigid elders unchangeably set in their ways is fair in a way, and unfair in a way. An older person is formed rather than flexible; and for that very reason may need less protection against upsetting novelty than some people assume. Young people may find their grandparents more tolerant and even appreciative of unconventional ways of life than their parents are able to be. Life has a shape already, and larger dollops can be added to the mixture without it curdling, like the later stages of making mayonnaise.

Old age as decay

Is the praise of old age running away with us? All this can be said about middle age.[7] Is fruition really a phenomenon of middle age, with the miseries of real aging still waiting for us? If the late twentieth century is really different from earlier times, maybe it is long active retirement which is new, with old age still what it was, though people reach it later and more people reach it. The more successfully medicine staves off bodily ills, the more aware we are of what medicine still cannot do. We still live in great uncertainty about how we shall end our days; and what does seem plain is that the human frame is not built to continue in vigour for much more than three score years and ten. It looks as if the stereotype of decay must be the right one after all.

Plenty of old people reach a stage beyond maturity, when their grey hairs may be honoured but their capacities diminish, their cherished ideas are of no account and they know or believe that they are at best a beloved nuisance. Optimisim is all very well, but looking on the bright side is not the answer to dementia, deafness, blindness, arthritis, helplessness, even repulsiveness; and worst of all the loneliness of outliving one's contemporaries. Browning's 'Grow old along with me, The best is yet to be . . .'[8] is not false but conditional. To grow old together is one of the great blessings of life; but to many people it is denied.

Realism does not require that we should anticipate all these ills. There may be sensible precautions to be taken, but bracing oneself to fight with shadows is not a sensible precaution. Every one of these troubles can afflict younger people too. Human beings at all ages are vulnerable creatures, so of course it is rare to reach old age without having acquired some 'thorn in the flesh'. To assume that to become old means that some particular dread, whether merely tiresome or agonizing, is bound to be fulfilled, is no more rational than to squander one's youth in imagining the disasters that can and do happen. Resignation to non-existent trouble is wasted. Future suffering can sometimes be circumvented; but only present suffering can be faced. We cannot know, when we are watching someone we love go downhill, whether it is worse to be senile oneself; but at least we need not add these distresses together and set ourselves to undergo old age at first and second hand both at once. To say ahead of time 'I don't mind so long as it's not *that*' can even hinder us from coping with *that*, if one day we meet it.

Old age as continuity in changing circumstances

The message from people with experience of long life is that they still feel the same: perhaps still in their twenties. The *Oxford Companion to the Mind* bears this out. 'The changes in personality can best be summed up by saying that old age is a revealing time, when the best and worst in us stand out in bold relief.'[9]

This is not surprising. Biologically speaking we are aging from birth. It was inaccurate to say that aging does not happen to everyone: the question is, when does it become an experience? Is it when the older generation begins to die, or sooner than that? The greying hair of one's parents is an early reminder of their mortality and one's own. Is it when the younger ones begin to take over one's role? For many people this happens with the arrival of a new sibling. Is 'You are a big boy now' so different from 'Remember your age'? Aging begins to be noticed when one is no longer able to do what one did. Finding oneself the oldest generation, seeing one's children begin to go grey, are parts of the same life story as outgrowing toys and leaving school.

A theological way of putting this is to say that all along we are living in the 'end-time'. Refraining from mapping out the future, accepting one's limitations, letting go of what one thought one possessed, and all this with a good grace, are not new lessons for the aged but are supposed to be the stuff of Christian life. Christians talk easily about self-denial, about 'dying daily' and being born again. What we grab we wreck; what we give up can be renewed; but living by this understanding is another matter. The path between self-indulgence and kill-joy renunciation is extremely narrow; but there is no need to let Nicodemus[10] suggest to us that it gets more difficult further on. Old age may show us how to let go, guiding our awkward hands like teaching children to write.

The lesson may be especially hard for women, conditioned as they have been to value themselves for their youth and beauty and to look on wrinkled age as a different form of life. There is a German Renaissance picture[11] of hideous old women plunging in a magic pool to regain their youth, which encapsulates this chronic fear. It is not alchemy which is really needed, but comprehension that inside every old person is the very same human being who once was young.

A more recent over-emphasis which makes aging frightening is the current one-sided cult of autonomy. To be 'dependent' is nearly as big a bogey as to be ugly. For some people it is a hard lesson to learn, to take and not be in a position to give. Again the stereotypes hinder: youth is to be active and confer benefits, age is to be patient and receive them. This contrast needs to be blurred. Human beings throughout their lives need to learn the true interplay of 'give and take', in which the giver is the gainer and the taker the benefactor. To allow one another, at all stages, the rewarding reciprocal pleasure of this interchange is the human meaning of grace. It is high time to rethink our notions about activity and passivity, striving and acceptance, strength and weakness, dignity and humility, energy and stillness, and indeed about work and play.[12] To see how all these contrasts properly apply to the whole of life could make the experience of aging less lonely and allow glimpses of the grace of God fulfilling the promise: '. . . even to your old age I am he, and to grey hairs I will carry you. I have made, and I will bear; I will carry and will save.'[13]

Notes

1. Cf. C. S. Lewis *The Screwtape Letters*, London 1942, Letter 6.
2. Teilhard de Chardin, *Le milieu divin*, London and New York 1960.
3. Shakespeare, *Macbeth*, Act V, Scene 3.
4. Shakespeare, *As You Like It*, Act II, Scene 7.
5. Psalm 128.6.
6. Shakespeare, *Richard II*, Act I, Scene 1.
7. I have indeed made some of these points, made here about 'aging', just over ten years ago in an article called 'Moral Choice', in *Change and Choice: Women and Middle Age*, ed. Beatrice Musgrave and Zoe Menell, London 1980.
8. Rabbi Ben Ezra.
9. *The Oxford Companion to the Mind*, ed. R. L. Gregory and O. I. Zangwill, Oxford 1987, p. 14.
10. John 3.4.
11. In the Dahlem Museum in Berlin.
12. W. H. Vanstone, *The Stature of Waiting*, London 1982, explores these themes inspiringly, especially if his discussion is taken in conjunction with his earlier book *Love's Endeavour, Love's Expense*, London 1977.
13. Isaiah 46.4.

Life as Full Flowering*

The Contribution of Older People to a Humane Civilization

Paul Schotsmans

Ethics and gerontology – for some people that is yet one more inauthentic extension of ethical concerns; for others it is a sign that ethics is keeping up with the times and is now already preparing for a situation which at all events will be a reality in the future. Ethics reflects on human beings and their striving for the good – indeed one might put it more strongly: their striving for happiness. It is concerned with questions like: how can men and women live and act so as to become authentically human? How do they arrive at the deepest mystery of their humanity so that life can eventually be lived in its full flowering?

Moreover ethicists do not cross any frontiers when they shift their attention to the world of older people. Here we have a very important phase of human life, and the ethical question 'How can the human be brought to fulfilment?' is more than ever appropriate. For older people tend either to be forgotten or to become the butt of sometimes very one-sided or dehumanizing judgments. To remain young has always been a human dream. Elixirs of youth were already peddled in classical times and in the Middle Ages. Even now there are still people who undergo all kinds of treatments for rejuvenation. When Romania was still the old Romania of the Ceaucescus, for many Westerners it was the land of cures *par excellence*. But did this realize the human in its fullness? Is this meaningful aging? Is deep freezing for dead bodies the solution to making the dream of eternal youth come true? Or is the answer the riches of a mysterious flowering of the later years of life with humanity?

Of course ethicists opt for the latter, at least if they want to give striving

*The author's use of the word *Vol-tooi-ing* at this point and elsewhere is impossible to render in English. It ordinarily means 'completion', 'fulfilment', but breaking it down into syllables as indicated by the hyphen brings out another word, *tooi*, which means adornment, decoration, array, and adds richness to the original composite.

for the good, as that which is fully human, a central place in ethical reflection. It is their task to give unabridged expression to the human, and to reflect critically on all attempts to reduce the rich kaleidoscope of the human mystery to pseudo-happiness. As a framework for this enterprise I would refer to the model of the ethics of responsibility. In my view what is humanly desirable is best described on the basis of three anthropological orientations: uniqueness, intersubjectivity and solidarity. In this article I want to apply these terms of reference to the appropriate situation of older people. Humanity in fullness is achieved when human beings can develop in relational openness to others and the Other and so can collaborate in a human society which is good to live in – for anyone, young or old! This becomes the anthropological framework within which at the same time I shall also indicate the lines on which I want to discuss the problem of older people in an attempt to provide a human perspective.

I. In search of an ethical approach to the problems of older people

So the person, the relationship and the wider community are the three values which form the basis for all others. Our complementary view of human nature implies an integral task for human happiness. The recognition of the uniqueness and originality of the individual, the keeping open of relations with a view to far-reaching and broadening human encounters and working in solidarity for a humane society each in themselves form an ethical programme. I want to stress once again that only by interweaving these vectors of becoming human can life develop into meaning and fulfilment. In the light of this reciprocal intertwining I now want also to relate the three basic orientations outlined above to older people and a meaningful way of growing older.

1. Personal fulfilment

The question here is that of the quality of being human which ultimately needs to be striven for if we are to talk of 'meaning-full-ness', with the stress on the 'full'. This is the question of the fullest possible quality of human dignity or the 'maximizing of humanity' (as W. Korff terms it).[1] With Ricoeur we can call this the question of what is humanly most desirable and the place or the way in which this quality of full humanity gets its best opportunities and possibilities; in other words, the way in which it can best be guaranteed and realized (though this does not automatically mean that it can in fact be thus realized in a qualitatively meaningful way).[2]

We find an interesting psychological point of contact for the search for an answer to the question of meaningfulness (or fulfilment in life, as I would prefer to call it here) in the Viennese psychiatrist Viktor Frankl.[3] In his view, human beings cannot be reduced to a striving for power (Adler) or a striving for pleasure (Freud); in addition to this there is also a will for meaningfulness. This comes about because the dynamic of human existence transcends the individual and stands judgment on what is other than itself: on something or someone, in other words on a meaning that must be fulfilled in a task or in love of another person. Human beings find fulfilment by devoting themselves to a meaning outside their own skin. The more they are taken up in a task, the more they are dedicated to others, the more human they become. Human existence is essentially transcendence of self and not realization of self, just as human beings ultimately do not want happiness in itself but a reason for being happy. Some people imagine self-realization and happiness to be side-effects of the striving for meaning, values or ideals. And from the moment that happiness and self-development are sought after for their own sake, they become unattainable. Freud already said that 'people are strong as long as they have strong ideas behind them'. This means that the other, or the meaning to which human beings need to turn if they are really to develop, must really imply fullness of meaning – again with the accent on the 'full'.

Here Frankl points out how many people in our society are bowed down by too few rather than too many demands. So people do not so much need an escape from tension as the stimulus of a potential meaningfulness, a goal which is literally worth 'the trouble' and which they need to fulfil. Thus people need what R. Burggraeve has so rightly called a dynamic of heights.

Many people ask whether this also applies to those who are older. Simone de Beauvoir herself asserted that the moralists want older people to be seized up in resignation rather than opened up towards a striving for meaningful goals in their last years: 'Those moralists who for political or ideological reasons vindicate old age claim that it frees the individual from his body.'⁴ Of course we leave to older people what they think of the moralists. For me, Frankl's thought is a perfect rendering of my interest in the unique older person and the possibilities which any aged person must seize on in order really to find a personal task. Indeed, it is striking how often radical defenders of self-realization and the idea of freedom think this orientation on a task essential for a meaningful old age. That is also true of Simone de Beauvoir, among others. She stresses in an impressive way that older people really must continue to aim at a goal, a task, a duty. Her monumental work on old age is one long plea that older people should not allow themselves to become seized up but should activate themselves and look for a meaningful project in life.

If old age is not an absurd parody of our former life, only one solution is possible and that is to go on pursuing ends that give meaning to our existence – devotion to individuals, to groups, to causes, social or political, intellectual or creative work.[5]

When her friend and great inspiration, J. P. Sartre, touches on the same theme, he comes to almost an identical conclusion: 'It is the future which decides whether the past is living or not.'[6] Orientation on the future – or on a project – is thus essential to making life meaningful. This insight is also expressed repeatedly in Anglo-Saxon literature. As an illustration here I simply refer to John C. Bennett, as he formulates the three ethical orientations for aging.[7] These are that society should do justice to older people (we shall return to this later), freedom, and finally responsibility. In connection with this last, among other things he indicates what this responsibility or this task can consist in:

I emphasize that they should have as much responsibility for the conditions of their lives, a sense of responsibility for the welfare of the elderly as a group, and responsibility for their immediate community and for the decisions, often political, of the larger society. Prior to all these moral concerns that touch the lives of the elderly is the need to overcome the stereotypes through which people so often see them and through which they so often see themselves.[8]

Responsibility is thus the key word. Here the specific tasks can be described in very concrete terms:

. . . to do what they can to improve the conditions under which elderly people live; other people should not limit themselves in their public activity to the issues that especially affect their welfare. A great many of them have a freedom that they did not have during their years of employment to act on the basis of new thinking about the institutions and policies of their society; local, regional, and national as well as cultural and political.[9]

What this amounts to is therefore that older people should help to improve the living conditions of their age group. At the same time they can use creatively the free time that they have to reflect critically on existing institutions and norm patterns and to make suggestions for the improvement of the living conditions in which their various societies exist. Bennett also thinks it most important of all that seniors should break through existing stereotypes or prejudices and that they themselves should contribute towards a change of mentality.

This indicates the fundamental basic attitude of fulfilment of life which I would be glad to see given greater substance. While one is well aware that older people live between two poles of life (the expectation of further meaningful and satisfying life on the one hand and the threat of dying on the other), it is important that they, too, continue to look for the way in which they can find a meaningful place in the world of people and things. They have in fact realized that in place of a hazy happiness there must be striving for satisfaction: in peaceful living with fellow men and women, unfulfilled society and oneself. But this being-at-peace must never develop into resignation; the contribution of older people to society consists in their demonstrating what is fundamentally human and standing up for these values. I shall go on to illustrate this at length. Here it may become clear that by still being involved in tasks, older people are at the same time involved in true fulfilment of life.

II. Life as full flowering in relationship with others and with God

So we can never be human alone. In essentials, as human beings we stand in an open relationship, related to the reality in which we live, to the other people to whom of course we owe our existence and who surround us, and to God. If we want to be fully ourselves, we need encounters with others, and in addition we also need to be 'encountered' by others. For older people the mystery of their happiness often lies in this relational interweaving of their existence. It would take us too far to discuss all relational networks. So I shall limit myself here to the aspects of living with a partner, with children and grandchildren, and with close relationships in society.

1. If we have happiness in life . . .

The quality of the relationship between husband and wife at a later stage of life is often determined by the quality of the history of the previous years of their lives, depending on whether or not these have been lived satisfyingly as a conversation between two partners. P. Nijs has rightly pointed out that a new myth has developed here. Whereas people used to talk about the sexless child, now there is a prevalent myth of the sexless older person.[10] Perhaps this myth can be explained by the fact that despite the contraceptive revolution of our twentieth century, sexuality still remains orientated on procreation. Of course a good deal of further reflection and research is necessary here. But it seems important to me that sexology and sexual ethics should not ignore this theme.

The patterns of values in our society keep evolving with enormous speed. Whereas earlier the older person was included in the network of the family and the extended family, now we are seeing a marked increase in small nuclear families or small-scale partner-relationships. Therefore the tabu of sexuality has to be broken at an older age. Here love can develop into a language without words. Experience shared over the years in good and bad days can undermine a relationship, but it can also deepen it: if the love can last so long, then it must be real love (as J. Brel remarks). It is perhaps one of the most apt expressions of 'the wordless understanding' which love between two old people can become after a process of maturing over the years.

However, when one partner dies, the surviving older person is often left alone. For most of such people there is no longer any place in family structures as they exist nowadays. As a result marriages of pensioners are becoming an increasingly frequent phenomenon: older people look for new partners in their age group in order to break out of the lonely forsakenness of their situation. In Belgium, however, there are often heavy fiscal penalties for marriage which make it materially impossible for many old people to have a legal wedding. To the degree that this is a restriction on their opportunities for development and meaningfulness, appropriate legislation should be passed. Indeed one could put it even more strongly. This change would be no more and no less than a real humanization of a legislation which needs to be altered so that older people, too, have the possibility of an honourable mode of existence. It seems absurd that marriage is made impossible because of a fiscal system. Such a law is unjust and needs to be humanized.

2. Children and grandchildren

One of the most special relationships for older people in Western countries at present is that between grandparents and grandchildren. Seldom has a future generation been so strongly prepared by the previous generation as now. Many people will recognize the image of rather elderly couples taking grandsons or granddaughters to school and bringing them home. All this is a result of the enormous pressure of our competitive society on people in middle age. Here older people again play a role of undeniable significance. They can bring equilibrium and tranquillity into the existence of their grandchildren. But not all this is accepted gratefully by many older people. Are they prepared for this task? At an earlier stage did they not devote their best energies to bringing up their own children? Does this still make sense, above all when the generation gap has become so great so quickly? Here, too, the structure of society leaves little room; so here too reflection is needed on the possibilities for humanizing this situation and changing it in a humane way.

As for relations with their own children, here of course we have problems with the way in which older people are accepted later in life. Here it would be a good thing to allow a grandparent to speak from personal experience.

A dream in life . . . To live at home as long as possible and to be healthy. To live at home with each other and to be able to remain healthy . . . When do we take precautions to ensure that we can remain in our home as long as possible? What agreements do we make? Husband, wife, children? And when? With a view to a happy and tranquil old age? In other words, with a view to a good quality of life when we become old? Here sadly enough we have to note that as long as we are both healthy and well off there are no problems and God's water is allowed to flow over God's fields day in, day out: parents and children. For in fact the quality of life is a family problem. Here the quality of life is like the fable of the grasshopper and the ant. It is a matter of foresight and family solidarity. Things can be made very much easier if they are tackled in time and discussed openly and realistically among all the parties concerned, i.e. parents and children.[11]

Central to this argument is the possibility of prior discussion. All too often people find themselves in a position of being taken by surprise through circumstances. Developing life as a project also implies trying to plan well, breaking through the tabu of old age and honestly making systematic arrangements. In this way one takes one's life in one's hands and relationships become the framework in which this life can flower.

3. A project between the generations

Finally, I also want to investigate a way in which the demands of existence can be integrated into a meaningful activity. Many older people complain of boredom, slavery to the TV, meaninglessness, etc. However, there can be so much to do in one's own street or neighbourhood, so much humanity to bring, that this complaint can sound almost hypocritical. Thus in Antwerp a local project has been started with older people, aimed at reducing the gap between the generations.[13] Older people look after their neighbours' children; they have also taken on responsibility for helping newly-discharged ex-prisoners on their first steps in freedom. Drug addicts who want to break the habit are offered the protection of an open and safe house. Young people with problems are taken in.

Of course such projects are aimed at vigorous older people. However, they do offer possibilities of contact between people of different ages and make society more human, because it is more open to all those who make it up.

For me such projects are, moreover, real incarnations of my view of a humanity with full dignity. Here people live out their being as relational, fully take responsibility on themselves and put themselves at the service of a task which brings to life an undiminished humanity.

III. The contribution of older people to a humane civilization

This third dimension of humanity brings us to the macro-ethical level of our reflections. What has been said so far has made it clear how strongly our society is subject to all kinds of developments. The place of the older person in society is certainly no longer so obvious. An illustration may clarify this: in Japan, which is confronted with the problem of aging to an even greater degree than Belgium, Mr Miti, the Minister of International Trade and Industry, proposed the solution of building holiday villages for older people abroad. The yen is a strong currency. All comforts have to be provided, so of course the industrialized countries are prime favourites. So not all the countries in the world were considered. The favourites were Australia, Argentina, Spain, Sri Lanka, France, the Philippines and Costa Rica. The first village was to be finished in 1992. That year also sees the celebration of the five hundredth anniversary of the discovery of America by Columbus, hence of course the name 'Silver Columbia'.

The story may sound somewhat fictitious, but the fact remains that as a society we face a very great challenge. Within the perspective of the history of the world's population, at the end of our twentieth century we are increasingly confronted with the problem of the population explosion. Typical of this phenomenon is the fact that more than sixty per cent of the world's population lives in Asia and Africa, areas where there is the most poverty and where malnutrition, illness, illiteracy and a short lifespan go hand in hand with inadequate technical and economic organization. In these countries the population explosion in turn leads to further and more serious underdevelopment, causes greater poverty, and cripples economic and social progress.

Europe – the old mother continent – is a clear exception here. The old continent is increasingly evolving towards a *status quo*. This development is bringing a marked decrease in its share of the world population: from fifteen per cent around 1950 to ten per cent in 1980 and only six per cent around 2025. The decline in the birth rate is of course playing the most important role here. Hence the population in Western countries no longer displays a pyramidal structure. Belgium is a clear example of this: the number of children today is declining even below what is increasingly becoming the norm of a family with two children.

On the other side of the continuum this is creating the problem of an aging population. The pattern of deaths has also changed: the maximum lifespan has not increased, but an increasing number of people achieve it, so that the average lifespan is rising. As a result of this shift, dying is concentrated at an older age: three out of every four deaths relate to this group, as contrasted with forty-three per cent in 1920.

Within the older age group itself a distinction is increasingly being drawn between the old and the very old, above all as a result of the increase in the latter group. In order to achieve international standardization, the World Health Organization already made this distinction in the 1960s. Because heterogeneity within the age group itself is so great, a further differentiation is also used. This produces three sub-groups within the aged population: the young group (60 to 69), the middle group (70 to 84) and the very old (85 and older).

This aging of our population in any case has a number of important social and economic consequences. It also causes material or psycho-social difficulties for a large number of people. From an empirical investigation on the basis of a representative survey it emerges that the aged are irrefutably in the worst situation as far as security of living conditions is concerned.[13] In itself this already raises ethical questions and calls for ethical analysis. However, the whole phenomenon is of such a kind as to confront present-day society with a new challenge, unprecedented and therefore sometimes surprising. All this calls for some reorientation in ethical thinking. New ways of living 'together' must be sought; furthermore, there is a need for a new just order in which the aged are given a legitimate place. Reflection on this lies within the sphere of ethics and so I shall go into it further.

1. A basic fact

A basic fact of human existence, that men and women are by definition social beings, compels us to live as a society. Directly bound up with this is the need and at the same time the opportunity for human creativity and responsibility. Human beings are capable of developing survival mechanisms within the framework in which they are born. They are open to the world and must become creators from it of their second nature, culture. In connection with the aged, one can present this task as follows: what is the right, the most just, attitude towards them? What place do they have within our society? These questions are certainly now becoming urgent: the issue is no longer 'How old does a person grow?', but 'How does a person grow old?'. If we take into account here that there is no such thing as 'the old person' and that no group is so heterogeneous as this age group, then we create an additional difficulty in the search for an adequate solution to the problem of a society with an increasing number of old people.[14]

The way in which the old have been approached hitherto has been defined by the predominant value system in a society. Here it is above all the younger generations who have given the old their place, status and role. The old themselves are now scarcely recognized. This has come about because Western industrial society formerly stressed the incapacity of the old rather than the experience that they have. In other societies we see the roles reversed, and the old are revered because of their rich experience and wise counsel, which still gives them an important part to play. Within industrialized society we see that once a person steps out of the round of work, he or she also steps out of what brings meaning and repute in this society, namely the process of production. That illustrates how much a particular priority of values – the importance of production and competition – determines attitudes to the aged.

At the same time, in this way we inevitably come up against an obstinate formulation of the initial question: 'What is the proper attitude towards the aged?' One might ask whether this is not the wrong place to start. What we have established as a basic fact, that men and women are by nature social beings, also applies to the aged. The question of a proper attitude to the aged then implies that everything must start from the perspective of others or society. Perhaps this is the heart of the problem, namely that society wants to answer for the aged, conditioned by the prevalent system of values to the view that they can no longer answer for themselves. The consequence of this is that the aged are no longer valued as people in their own right and moreover can no longer act competently. But that is to disparage them rather than respect them.

2. An alternative which is faithful to humanity

In my view, in fact people are always too inclined to begin from the question of what society can do for the aged. If we question this sequence, we automatically come to the issue of power: who is taking the helm? This may become clear if we turn the question the other way round: a society which was dominated only by the aged would seem to most of us to be an unjust society. Living as a society presupposes that everyone can have a share in bearing responsibility. This implies the task of arriving at social contracts which do justice to both parties: instead of exclusively starting from society – What can it do for the aged? – it would therefore be good to ask: What can the aged contribute to society? For what can they bear specific responsibility? In that case society becomes a two-way process: living together in the fullest and richest sense of the term.

So we must not be misled by an egocentric tendency in our society as a result of which someone is perceived as having value only if he or she is involved in productive work. This would be to misunderstand a fundamental characteristic of our existence: these people have worked in the world in which we live and because of this history we at least owe them due respect. Therefore society will only be able to integrate the aged authentically when we also learn to 'live together' instead of living next door to one another. A shift of mentality is needed here, or we shall find ourselves in the excesses of Dutch society, where for the sake of convenience people are taking refuge in the solution of euthanasia. Japan, too, has some special instances of this.

3. Also and above all a task for the aged

Of course this will require effort from both parties. On the one hand society will need to reverse its value system relating to the aged, and perhaps this will primarily call for a reversal of value judgments on society generally. The insights which have been acquired within the geronto-logical sciences have made a major contribution here. This information needs to be brought to the attention of the younger generations.

But the aged can also – indeed above all – be creative in the search for new – and more just – social contracts: for example they can experiment with new life-styles for the benefit of generations still to come. If people want society to look at them afresh and respect them, they have to show that they are worthy of this respect. A good relationship is at best reciprocal: this calls for the readiness of the old to defend themselves against the prejudices which are still widespread in society. However, they can only succeed in defending themselves against these prejudices if they also succeed as far as possible in breaking out of dependence.

In this sense a just hierarchy is one which begins from the view that it is best for the aged to live independent lives, for them to remain as independent as possible, and rely on outside help as a secondary stage. Those old people who are not independent are best looked after in families: this is a good opportunity for handing on rich experiences to people which will help them to face the future. Only if this is impossible should an institution be considered.

Conclusion

I think that this threefold orientation offers an approach to the problems of older people which is faithful to our humanity. Whenever a new lifestyle is introduced, one must investigate whether the independence of the aged is furthered, or whether the relational possibility of a mutual enrichment is realized and whether the aged can truly live together with other groups in society. The ethicist above all stresses the values of independence, relational creativity and solidarity. This runs counter to the attitudes of rejection, prejudice and selfishness which are increasingly coming into the foreground. However, it seems important that the younger generations are aware of this: they cannot guarantee themselves any future worth living if they leave isolated and distressed the pillars of the world in which they live.

It is true that old age is the time of life in which activity and activism diminish, to make way for a greater tendency towards remembering and contemplation. But I have sought to plead for the enlivening of the relationships in which older people can come alive: relationships with themselves, with others, with society and with God. In this way the garland of years can be formed and become a laurel wreath of the goodness in human existence.

Translated by John Bowden

Notes

1. W. Korff, *Theologische Ethik. Eine Einführung*, Freiburg 1975.
2. P. Ricoeur, 'Le problème du fondement de la morale', *Sapienza* 28, 1975, 313–37.
3. V. Frankl, *De wil zinvol te leven*, Rotterdam 1980, 22–7.
4. Simone de Beauvoir, *Old Age*, Harmondsworth 1977, 351.
5. Ibid., 601.
6. Ibid., 404.
7. J. C. Bennett, 'Ethical Aspects of Aging: Justice, Freedom, and Responsibility', in J. E. Thornton and E. R. Winkler, *Ethics and Aging*, Vancouver 1988, 41–53.
8. Ibid., 41f.
9. Ibid., 46f.
10. P. Nys, *De eenzame samenspelers*, Kapellen 1976.
11. A. E. Craenen, 'De kwaliteit van leven. Een grootouder spreekt uit eigen ervaring', in J. P. Baeyens (ed.), *Proceedings of the Ninth Winter Meeting Oostende. Gerontologie en Geriatrie 1986*, Louvain 1987, 159–64.
12. Lieve Vandekerckhoven, *Werkgroep Ten Leven*, Vita et Pax, Antwerp.
13. H. Deleeck, J. Berghman, P. van Heddegem and L. Vereycken, *De Sociale Zekerheid tussen droom en daad*, Deventer 1980.
14. Hilde van den Hooff, *De veroudering van de bevolking. Een nieuw fenomeen – een nieuw antwoord*, unpublished thesis, Louvain Theology Faculty 1988.

A Spirituality of Aging

Eugene C. Bianchi

I want to address one of the more neglected areas in the field of aging, namely, a spirituality for older persons. The extraordinary growth of aging populations, especially in technologically-advanced countries, is well known. This growth, however, enhances the importance of my topic. Considerable progress has been made in medicine, nutrition, housing, transportation, law and other realms relative to gerontology. But these admirable developments have not been matched in theology, philosophy and ethics. Thinkers in these areas, and in the humanities generally, have not sufficiently explored the deeper dimensions of aging.

A spirituality for older persons

Spirituality has to do with issues of depth and significance in human life. I would like to explore such a spirituality in terms of middle age and of elderhood. In general, mid-life extends from about age forty to age sixty; elderhood, the period after sixty, can be divided in various ways, e.g., the young old and the old old. My approach, therefore, is developmental in terms of different life stages. It is a mistake to think that there are only two seasons, youth and adulthood, as though the latter were a plateau of sameness. Mid-life has its special challenges and special opportunities for deeper spiritual growth; so also does elderhood. Moreover, a spirituality for aging should ideally begin during the middle years, for it is then that we encounter experientially our own mortality. If we do not begin to grapple with our own aging in mid-life, we may find it much harder in later years to turn our losses into gains in terms of spiritual development.

I consider the spirituality of aging to be a form of religiousness. I am not referring to traditional religions, although the myth and ritual of the latter can be very helpfully applied to crucial aging experiences. Rather, I am pointing to a religiousness intrinsic to negotiating life passages with their opportunities for deeper discernment and commitment. For example, gradually coming to grips in a creative way with one's own mortality is a major life task. It usually requires years of reflection, self-struggle, increasing self-esteem, and a willingness to risk one's whole life adventure. This can be a profound religious experience in the very process of our aging. As we shall see, this requires a kind of faith and hope at the very heart of life transitions in mid-life and elderhood.

Sub-themes in my approach to the spirituality of aging are societal and ethical. Modern technological society militates against the kind of reflectiveness I am proposing for those in middle age. A fuller spirituality calls for opening contemplative spaces and times in a busy life. But technological culture drives middle-aged persons into intense and competitive action. Opening contemplative spaces in our lives is possible, but very difficult. It is not rewarded or even encouraged by dominant economic and political systems. Thus mid-life spirituality cuts against the grain of the culture. Furthermore, my vision for elderhood spirituality also defies the general intention of technological culture. I envision elders who have worked through the transitions of mid-life becoming even more intensely concerned about great human issues of ecology, peace and justice. Such elders would return, in different ways, to the centres of decision-making and of service. But technological culture pushes the old to the periphery of society, encouraging them to live out their 'golden years' in pursuits of individualistic consumerism.

Aging and altruism

Thus this spirituality of aging has an ethical or moral component. Elders who have worked through the crises of mid-life and older age, and who have made peace with their own mortality, will be inclined towards lives of greater altruism. They experience a gradual *metanoia*, or change of heart, that comes from confronting personal losses in the life cycle. This can result in a person fashioning a different ethical value system. Rather than focusing mainly on increasing personal wealth and enhancing one's ego by accumulating power over others, the elder of deeper spirituality will have learned to empathize with and alleviate suffering in the world. He or she will become sensitized to wider ethical concerns in local communities and in global situations. I am not referring to an ethical consciousness deriving from books or teachers, however helpful these may be. I am stressing rather the development of virtues such as a sense of justice and benevolence that are learned in the course of negotiating existential transitions in one's own life. Often these transitions involve suffering and loss in very concrete ways. For example, the loss of youth in mid-life and the loss of a spouse or friend in elderhood.

Of course, such movement from egocentrism to altruism is not automatic in the aging process. For a variety of reasons, psychological and cultural, many people remain stuck in the narrow ethics of a totally self-centred individualism. Others are embittered by life's challenges and losses. Such elders close themselves off from the ethical patterns of altruistic care and service. Old people can become paranoid, inflexible and harsh. Sometimes these negative attitudes are defences against experiencing more personal pain. For some people, therefore, the challenges of aging can become opportunities for spiritual and ethical growth, while for others the same experiences foster selfish regression and attitudes of social hostility.

It is impossible to discuss adequately here why people age in such different ways from an ethical point of view. But in trying to understand the unfolding of an ethical spirituality of aging we can explore the crucial areas of 1. self-understanding, 2. one's life work(s), and 3. relationships with others and with nature.

Self-understanding. The central problem of middle age is the existential confrontation with one's own mortality. Death is, of course, understood in youth, but not often as 'my death'. This sense of mortality is frequently spoken about as loss of youth. In a spirit of contingency, one begins to calculate one's years not from the beginning but from the end. This may be experienced as a feeling of restricted time. Many follow cultural dictates to distract themselves from dealing directly with these sentiments. The midlife self may also grieve the death of youthful dreams. He or she may feel anew the psychological wounds and guilts of childhood, problems that may have been suppressed in young adulthood to conform to society's demands to find an occupation and start a family. In this enhanced state of personal contingency, long-held values and beliefs may weaken.

From the perspective of spiritual-ethical growth, the self in mid-life stands on the threshold of personal transformation. In a paradoxical manner, the more one faces and accepts 'necessary losses', the more one is opened to the exercise of enabling power inwardly and outwardly. The ego can be gradually transformed away from a stance of competitive, domineering power (a 'natural' outcome of self-preservation tendencies in an insecure world). This process is a religious one in which the ego lets go, releases some of its defences, allowing God's benevolent, gracious presence amid sufferings and joys to enter one's being. Rather than a single religious conversion, this process of aging in depth comprises a series of conversions in the face of challenges inherent in or related to the aging cycle. Such moments of self-realization will be occasioned by different events. Some will be brought to these liminal states by physical or mental sufferings; others by happenings in the family or the outside world. From a spiritual and ethical viewpoint, these moments of transformation are crucibles for change in self-understanding. Dialogue with one's unconscious during such times in a contemplative environment can be of immense value.

A gradual change in self-understanding is usually marked by attitudes concerning truth, power and love. The quest for truth broadens, expanding beyond the overly confining truths of family, class, religion and nation. This does not mean an abandonment of discerning intellect, but rather an emancipation of mind that refuses to bring facile closure to novel ideas and happenings. Such aging people portray a more adventurous and risking cast of thought. The change concerning power, as noted above, means the embracing of enabling power in place of dominative power. The latter is coercive and self-serving; the former, persuasive and benevolent, wanting the welfare of the other. The aging enabler exercises the power of an authentic mentor, encouraging freedom in others. In an ideal progression along the stages of aging, such a person becomes an ever more loving being. Such love has little to do with popular romanticism. Rather, it means a deeper bonding, through empathetic compassion, with the lot of humanity and nature. Such elders, in mid-life and later, move in their innermost selves towards being world citizens, pondering and promoting the general welfare. Although certain celebrated personalities manifest this self-understanding in later life, many lesser-known people show it in non-publicized and local circumstances.

The period of elderhood offers possibilities for continuing this growth in self-understanding. The confrontation with real and potential losses takes on a special cast for many in the later stages of aging. A technological, youth-oriented society surrounds these elders with negative stereotypes about being old. Often there are increased physical disabilities among the elderly. Poignant losses of intimates and friends occur through death. The elderly self can also experience loss of worth after retirement from work. Such common events of the aging process become opportunities for the kind of growth mentioned in the paragraph above, a kind of 'growth through diminishment' (Teilhard de Chardin). Or these aging experiences constrict the spirit into bitterness, clinging and negativity. Such damaged elders cannot become ethical, spiritual models for the young, who must eventually face similar life crises. Yet we find outstanding examples of spiritually and ethically aware elders, even in very difficult life conditions. Such old people are the peacemakers, the wise ones whose wisdom and service society sorely needs. They are the ones whose voices must be heard again in the centres of decision-making.

World of Work. It is well known in modern psychology that one's work or various life endeavours constitute a vital source of self-esteem. In mid-life, a person may be at the high point of a career and yet be dissatisfied with his or her work. One's occupation may no longer bring the fulfilment it once did. One may have a sense of failure for not having achieved according to the dictates of society. There may be boredom and a feeling of being stuck in a given job. New problems face women in mid-life when they consider returning to the world of work after their children have left home. Moreover, millions of people are either unemployed or underemployed. Others work in oppressive and unhealthy conditions for inadequate incomes.

A spirituality of aging in this realm would flow from an appreciation of one's work as an extension of divine creativity in the world. From a philosophical-theological point of view, human work becomes part of the evolutionary development of creation, when such energies are not employed in destructive ways. We become co-partners with God in what A. N. Whitehead called the 'creative advance'. But we must relate this positive, theoretical spirituality to the practical problems mentioned above.

For more privileged people, an answer to some work-related problems may lie in the direction of rethinking the goals of their work in mid-life. They can envision their tasks in the mode of mentors. The mentor finds meaning in enhancing the well-being of the protégé without dominating the latter. The mentoring role is an exercise in benevolence that enriches both teacher and student. In a wider perspective, a mid-life person may be able to see work as a contribution to building a better human-natural community. For others in middle age, the work situation may not be sufficiently adaptable to new insights and needs. These persons sometimes need to take the risk of changing to other endeavours for their spiritual welfare. Lack of sustaining and significant work for a very large portion of the planet's people presents one of the most difficult problems facing humanity today. Fuller solutions of these problems encompass social and economic justice, political freedom, population control and ecological balance. A spirituality of aging, therefore, calls upon those in mid-life, especially persons in more privileged situations, to see solutions to problems in the world of work on both personal and societal levels.

Elderhood presents special problems because of retirement. For many in technological society, retirement from work engenders psychological and spiritual difficulties. In earlier times and non-Western cultures, an older person might continue to find meaning in advisory roles in a civilization of rural, extended families. But in the West today, the retiree is frequently cut off, perhaps in his or her sixties, from the world of work that made one feel significant. Education in mid-life for satisfying involvements after retirement is much needed. The whole concept of retirement as the end of one's work life needs rethinking. If the human life-span calls for personally-satisfying and community-contributing work from childhood to old age, new ways must be found to develop the potentials for working in old age. This work may take many forms, whether done for financial gain or not. In general, a spirituality of aging would summon the elder to seek occupations that are not only personally satisfying, but also socially valuable. Society needs the skills, experience and wisdom of elderly populations. Technological culture, with its premium on youthful vigour, wastes the talents of the old to its own detriment.

Relationships to persons and nature. In the area of intimacy and friendship, mid-life persons encounter perplexing questions. Men may feel uneasy about declining sexual potency, or they may experience a lack of intimacy in married life. Moreover, men in our culture, bred to compete for success in the marketplace, usually do not cultivate friendships with other men. The ensuing strain can lead to marital stress and to moribund relationships that drag on for ulterior motives. An ageist (ageism means discrimination based on being older) society causes women to be concerned about the loss of youthful beauty. Television advertisements, for example, continually give such messages, declaring that being over forty is a negative condition. Beneath such problems, men and women in mid-life may be seeking compensatory role reversals. For example, a man may want to cultivate the 'softer' emotions, and a woman may need to exercise assertiveness. Middle-agers are also often 'sandwiched' between the competing needs of children on the one side and elderly, sometimes frail, parents on the other.

Yet in a spirituality of aging, these problematic areas of mid-life also bring opportunities for personal renewal and growth. If middle-aged persons learn to cultivate contemplative times and spaces, they can find inner resources and new meaning from wellsprings within themselves. Mid-life offers occasions for deepening our friendships. We can better understand our limits and vulnerabilities, as well as the authentic needs of others. We may for the first time recognize the other as other, and not merely as an extension of our own desires. In brief, by working through the losses and other challenges of mid-life, we can learn to love more altruistically, to spend more time nourishing friendships and building community. Thus the outcome of this inner and interpersonal work can be a heightened ethical sensibility.

As noted above, elderhood brings special challenges that have an impact on relationships. But these very difficulties, even the loss of spouse and friends, can have a purifying and enlightening effect for those who have learned to be open to nature's transitions in the aging process. Such elders will display less egotism, even while they experience greater self-esteem. For they will have come to love themselves from within. They will manifest a simplicity and truthfulness concerning the world. They will be able to satisfy unmet needs of their own personalities, doing things that were neglected earlier in life. From their own diminishments, they will derive greater humility and compassion. An ideal for these elders can be summed up in the phrase 'stewardship for all life'. Instead of closing in on their own limits, they will embrace wider concerns, seeking to be of service to future generations.

Again, a spirituality of aging that leads people to cope in depth with losses and challenges that are part of the aging process will focus on the creative or learning potential of these very problematic areas. An expanded ethical consciousness will result. Such elders will choose to foster important movements for human betterment, such as causes for human rights, for the elmination of war, of hunger, and of crass social injustices. The ecologically perilous situation of the planet calls for such elders to become advocates for ecological sanity and harmony. Elderhood can be a time for special bonding with the animal and natural worlds. In youth we tend to be ego-centred as we foster our individual projects, often oblivious of our connection to the ecosystem. The very challenges of aging remind us that we are part of an evolving natural order. We experience our kindredship with the seasonal cycles of nature. The experience of bonding anew with animals, birds, trees and rivers constitutes an essential precondition for developing a creative ecological ethic. Otherwise, our ecological morality tends to be distant, conceptual and overly instrumental. Many aspects of this ethical growth through the diminishments of aging will be orchestrated in quiet and local modes.

This sketch of a spirituality for aging uncovers possibilities for older persons to grow inwardly, interpersonally, and communally. Such elders have a future in the quality aspects of the time remaining to them. They will live on in those whom they have helped, and they will hope to live on in God. These older people will not allow themselves to be hurled into a solitary existence on the periphery of society. They will return to the centres of decision-making, bring their skill and wisdom to benefit others. Every nation and community has models for emulation in this kind of older person. Such elders encourage us to enter the physically downward curve of life with hope for genuine spiritual ascent in our final seasons.

Aging, Suffering and Dying: A Christian Perspective

Walter J. Burghardt

For anyone in a developed country who lives a normal number of years, aging is inevitable. Not just growing older, but growing old, experiencing that for which we have only a frightening term: old age. There is no universal definition of old age: it begins much earlier in Burundi than in Britain. To set the parameters of my presentation, let me describe aging in a way that stresses the experience of developed countries: old age sets in when I sense that, after the usual periods of adolescence, young adulthood, and middle age, I am reaching the last significant stage of my life. Call it the winter of human existence; assume, with some recognized scholars, that it begins at roughly sixty to sixty-five. I shall 1. set up some of the problems the aged face; 2. link these to suffering and dying; 3. propose a perhaps surprising antidote to counteract the distressful aspects of aging.

I

Problems

Even apart from external circumstances, in the very best of situations, old age demands profound reflection. I must face up to Erik Erikson's key polarity: integration versus despair. Somehow I must grasp my life as something whole. I must come to terms with suffering: a body that is breaking down, illnesses to which aging flesh and spirit are especially heir. I must confront death: my own and the almost daily demise of dear ones.

In the United States, aging is complexified by a cultural phenomenon: the ideal of old age that America has fashioned. We inhabit a culture that canonizes youth and beauty, activity and productivity, power and sexual prowess. If you are eternally young and ceaselessly attractive, if after sixty or sixty-five you continue your career with little let-down and still make an impact on an acre of God's world, if you can jog or play squash or straddle a Honda, if you can still satisfy a man or woman sexually, then your aging is ideal. In fact, you're not growing old at all! The only ideal of old age we accept in the States is an aging without change or limits or loss.

Perhaps the most critical aspect of this problem is that the culture considers the elderly useless. By and large, the aged are seen as serving no particularly practical purpose: for family life (save perhaps as unpaid baby-sitters), for political life (save for a healthy Ronald Reagan), for industrial life. Knowledge and wisdom come from computers, not from tradition; from the creative imagination of the young and the restless, not from the hoary reminiscences of the ancients. Increasingly the young and the restless drive the senior partners into early retirement. And so many of the aged are a drain on the economy. Medicare, like the military, pushes the national budget into the trillions. The young are burdened with support of the old. Already doctors are toying with lethal injections for the comatose, the despairing, the useless. Simone de Beauvoir phrased it in a more general context with a pungent brevity:

> Apart from some exceptions, the old man no longer *does* anything. He is defined by an *exis*, not by a *praxis*: a being, not a doing. Time is carrying him towards an end – death – which is not *his* and which is not postulated or laid down by any project. This is why he looks to active members of the community like one of a 'different species', one in whom they do not recognize themselves.[1]

Precisely here is where the Christian vision, if not every Christian, records a resounding minority vote. Save for the unalterably comatose or the hopelessly senile or the indefinitely demented, there is no person alive who is 'finished', who has reached either perfection or the limit of his or her striving. A Christian is a pilgrim. Not simply because on this earth he or she has no lasting city, must echo the anonymous early Christian *Epistle to Diognetus*: '[Christians] take part in everything as citizens and put up with everything as foreigners. Every foreign land is their home, and every home a foreign land.'[2] More pertinently because Christian existence is a ceaseless following of Christ, a wondrous and fearful effort to get to be in his image, and that is a struggle that never ends this side of the grave.

This movement into Christ demands as an essential ingredient a kenosis, a self-emptying akin to Christ's own in taking our flesh. Kenosis is not a virtue requested from the Lord on one's retirement from active existence. All through life Christians have to 'let go': let go of where they've been, let go of the level of life where they are now, so as to live more fully. Let go of childhood and adolescence, of good looks and youthful energy, of familiar places and beloved faces, of a high-paying job and human applause, of self-righteousness and self-sufficiency. Not simply because we must, because we have no choice. Rather because only by letting go of yesterday can we grow more fully into Christ today. We do not *forget* our yesterdays; we simply dare not *live* in them.

Especially for the aging, kenosis, letting go, reaches a critical stage in suffering and dying.

II

Suffering/Dying

Suffering – pain of spirit, pain of flesh – is not limited to the aging. Before he was thirty, Beethoven began to experience the deafness that would induce his intense spiritual crisis. Born with multiple sclerosis, Christy Brown, author of *My Left Foot*, could use only that small member to paint and to compose. Short-story writer Flannery O'Connor, afflicted with lupus, died at thirty-nine. John Merrick, the horribly deformed 'elephant man' of stage and screen, left us at twenty-six. In our time AIDS victims are frighteningly young. Still, it is the aging who suffer Shakespeare's 'fardel of never-ending misery' precisely because of their age.

Suffering at any age is not easy for the human mind to understand. Even for those who have grown up with a God whose very name is Goodness and Love, much human suffering makes little or no sense: fifty million foetuses dead each year before birth, infants with Downs' syndrome, a good woman comatose for seven years, whole families killed in auto accidents, seven million Jews destroyed in the Holocaust – the mysteries are endless. The Jews of the Old Testament at times traced suffering to sin – the sin of parents, the sin of the nation, one's own sin. But even here there was no 'answer'. The Jews still asked why the ways of the wicked 'prosper at all times' (Ps. 10.5), consoled themselves that 'the fool and the stupid alike must perish and leave their wealth to others' (Ps. 49.10), could not help complaining, 'Has God in his anger shut up his compassion?' (Ps. 77.8). Job, confronted with innocent suffering, found human wisdom bankrupt, came face to face with a God who refused to enlighten his mind and simply appealed to Job's love and his trust.

Suffering, especially in the aging, calls not only for faith but for a spirituality. All Christian spirituality is the response of a man or woman to God revealing divine love through Christ in the Spirit. In the concrete, it consists in knowing, loving and serving God and God's children in the context of a community of faith, hope and love. Christian spirituality is a new, intimate relationship with the Blessed Trinity, a sharing in God's own life, a conscious experience of Love that thrusts us out from church to world in service to the very least of Christ's sisters and brothers. At its core, Christian spirituality is human love responding to divine love, to a God who 'so loved the world that he gave his only Son' (John 3.16), not only to share our flesh but to experience our pain and die our death. It is St Paul's passionate outburst, 'I have been crucified with Christ; it is no longer I who live, but Christ who lives in me; and the life I now live in the flesh I live by faith in the Son of God, who loved me and gave himself for me' (Gal. 2.20).

Here the mystery of suffering is not so much explained as enriched by another mystery, Paul's assertion that through suffering we 'complete in [our] flesh what is lacking in Christ's afflictions for the sake of his body, that is, the Church' (Col. 1.24). To plumb that mystery-laden affirmation, we the aging would do well to meditate on the dying which Karl Rahner described so eloquently in his last years as he focused ever more intensely on 'the cross . . . erected over history'.[3] What Paul phrased so baldly and economically – '[Christ Jesus] humbled himself with an obedience that meant death, even death on a cross' (Phil. 2.8) – Rahner expanded in a packed and poignant paragraph:

> According to Scripture we may safely say that Jesus in his life was the *believer* . . . and that he was consequently the one who hopes absolutely and in regard to God and men the one who loves absolutely. In the unity of this triplicity of faith, hope and love, Jesus surrendered himself in his death unconditionally to the absolute mystery that he called his Father, into whose hands he committed his existence, when in the night of his death and God-forsakenness he was deprived of everything that is otherwise regarded as the content of a human existence: life, honour, acceptance in earthly and religious fellowship, and so on. In the concreteness of his death it becomes only too clear that everything fell away from him, even the perceptible security of the closeness of God's love, and in this trackless dark there prevailed silently only the mystery that . . . has no name and to which he nevertheless calmly surrendered himself as to eternal love and not to the hell of futility . . . [I]n the last resort what happens in death is the same for all: we are deprived of everything, even of ourselves; we all fall, each of us alone, into the dark abyss where there are no further ways. And this death – which in the first place is simply ours – Jesus died; he who came out of God's glory did not merely descend into our human life, but also fell into the abyss of our death, and his dying began when he began to live and came to an end on the cross when he bowed his head and died.[4]

Therefore what? From one perspective we can conclude: Jesus died as we die, followed in our way. And so death must be 'emptied of final despair and futility'.[5] Important, exciting, comforting; but far more significant, more electrifying, more consoling is the other side of the coin. We can die as Jesus died, can follow in his way. It makes all the difference in the world. For Jesus did not simply die; he 'died into his resurrection'.[6] His human reality was finally accepted into the very life of God – for ever.

But Jesus' death-unto-resurrection does not change our dying automatically. We must accept freely 'this opportunity of dying with him as a beginning of life'.[7] Our task is to transform sheer similarity in dying to genuine following, transmute pure punishment for sin into a loving acceptance of God's life, murmur without reservation, 'Father, into your hands I entrust my spirit' (Luke 23.46). It calls for my supreme act of faith. For my death-unto-resurrection is not something I can verify empirically. I die not with an unassailable syllogism but with a lively hope. Here, too, I follow Jesus. A stunning truth: for all that he was God, this man too died not with experience of resurrection but with faith in his Father, with hope for life without end.

Dying with Jesus, however, dying *like* Jesus is not limited to the close of our earthbound existence, to the terminal cancer, the cardiac arrest. Dying in a theological sense begins when living begins; we share in Jesus' dying through the whole of our lives. Whatever makes for pain – pain of flesh or of spirit – should be part and parcel of our Christian dying. Diverticula or disappointments, schizophrenia or the wrenching of my heart, dying hopes or the death of a dear one, the insecurities of youth and the trembling of the aging – whatever it is that pricks my pride, assails my lustiness, intimates my mortality, takes the joy from my very bones – in all these brief moments of what Rahner called 'dying in instalments',[8] we confront the critical question, how are we to cope with them? Protest? Despair? Cling all the more frantically to what has not yet been snatched from us? Or accept each breakdown, not simply with resignation, with passivity, but with gratitude, as a grace from God?

Such active acceptance enters into the very definition of death. Now death ceases to be something that 'happens' to us. For all its dark side – 'a breaking of the whole human person, an unacceptable and repugnant event, disintegration rather than achievement, a final fall into the weakness of being human'[9] – death for a Christian should not be an experience I endure but an act I personally perform, a yes, an 'I do'. *I die*. Like the final cry of Jesus, my 'Into your hands' is an affirmation of life. Here, if anywhere, human existence finds integration. All the bitter-sweet of earthly living is brought together and offered to God in my most radical act of faith, my supreme act of confidence, my act of love without parallel. I die only to live!

III

Antidote

So profound a spirituality of aging does not come easily, is not infused with infant baptism. But neither does it arrive automatically at sixty-five. How, then, is it achieved? I propose what I announced above as a surprising antidote to the distressful effects of aging. After five decades of intense searching, my solution is: through contemplation. Contemplation in this context I conceive the way the Carmelite William McNamara described it: a long loving look at the real. Each word is crucial.

The *real* here is not an abstraction, an intangible God-in-the-sky. Reality is whatever *is*: things (snow-capped Alps, a ruddy glass of Burgundy, ocean waves, Notre Dame of Paris), vegetative life (a blade of grass, a rose of Sharon, a giant redwood, a luscious nectarine), the animal and avian world (a gentle doe, the carnivorous lion, the sweet-singing nightingale, an eagle in graceful flight), situations (war and peace, poverty and riches, joy and sorrow, living and dying), the realm of persons (newborn child, AIDS victim, dearest of kin, the compassionate Christ, God Three in One).

This real I *look* at. No longer do I analyse or argue it, describe or define it; I am one with it. I do not move around it; I enter into it. Not only my mind, cold reason; I am most myself, most human, most contemplative when my whole person responds to the real – eyes and ears, smelling and touching and tasting. Eyes meet, a bird's trill greets the dawn, a breeze caresses my cheek, the breath of cancer assails my nostrils, God speaks – and the whole man, the whole woman, comes alive.

This look at the real is a *long* look. Not so much hours or days; rather, resting unhurriedly (but not listlessly) in the real. I mean when time is irrelevant, when all that matters is this landscape of Matisse, this word of the Lord, this aroma of spaghetti Bolognese, this touch of a helpless hand, this taste of honey.

But this look at the real must be a *loving* look. It demands that the real captivate me, at times delight me. At times. For the real that is *Swan Lake* is not the real of Vietnam or the Persian Gulf; the dance that delights is not the blood that disgusts. For the real includes AIDS and abortion, apartheid and MS, bloated bellies and stunted minds, respirators and last gasps. But even here the real I contemplate must end in compassion, and compassion that mimics Christ is another word for love.

Have I been distracted from the aging? Quite the contrary. All our expensive efforts to ease the effects of aging will prove petty bromides unless the elderly can move through kenosis to contemplation – in fact, to kenosis through contemplation. It demands that society create a new climate – social and economic, political and psychological – where the aging can be freed to grow interiorly. Not by band-aid remedies: games calculated to pass the time, gardening that occupies my hands but bores my spirit, TV where I live a vicarious existence. Rather, a climate such that I can grow in oneness with God and with all that God has so lavishly fashioned, can look at things and 'the other' with laughter and compassion, can rejoice and be glad because *this* day of my life the Lord has made. Because *I* am alive!

Notes

1. Simone de Beauvoir, *The Coming of Age*, New York 1973, 322–3.

2. *Epistle to Diognetus* 5.5 (translated Kleist, Ancient Christian Writers 6, 139).

3. Karl Rahner, *Schriften zur Theologie* 15, *Wissenschaft und christlicher Glaube*, Zurich 1983, 20.

4. Karl Rahner, 'Following the Crucified', *Theological Investigations* 18, *God and Revelation*, New York and London 1983, 157–70: 165–6. I am deeply indebted to this remarkably theological and pastoral article for my basic insights on suffering and dying.

5. Ibid., 166.

6. Ibid.

7. Ibid., 167.

8. Cf. ibid., 169–70.

9. Bartholomew J. Collopy, 'Theology and the Darkness of Death', *Theological Studies* 39, 1978, 22–54: 39. Here Collopy is reproducing lineaments of the dark model.

Old People in the Church

The Subject Option in Old Age

Martina Blasberg-Kuhnke

I. The church and its elderly members

1. The state churches in the Federal Republic of Germany – an example

'The church should be concerned about the old,'[1] was one of the most emphatically expressed expectations of members of Protestant churches in an investigation which was carried out in the Federal Republic of Germany in 1968. Other subsequent sociological investigations point in the same direction: the churches form a social entity, perhaps *the* social entity, among whose urgent tasks is acceptance of the old.[2]

These expectations seem to be matched by a reality in the church. The churches are involved in the three central areas of social work with the old. They maintain, for example, two-thirds of all old people's homes and nursing homes in the Federal Republic through their welfare organizations Caritas and Diakonisches Werk, and a large number of the local social centres which on the whole look after old people in need of less care; they are therefore important supporters of *help for the old*. The *education of the old* has come to be established in recent years in the context of church adult education as an independent and steadily growing sphere, and almost every church community can point to *pastoral work among the old* in groups, clubs or even day centres. So the basic framework for relations between the churches and their elderly members looks favourable: the churches are to become committed in the sphere of social work with the old and to a large extent they live up to this expectation.

2. The old between commitment and a lack of esteem

However, under the surface of the institutional safeguarding of the church's involvement in work with the old and the pastoral care of the old, there is a significant number of unassimilated and unresolved questions and problems which highlight the reciprocal relationship between community, churches and old people as an area which is full of tension and subject to conflict.

First of all there is a clear discrepancy between the commitment of older members of the community, particularly older women, and the esteem that they experience. The greatest pastoral efforts are directed towards addressing and reaching the young and young adults; the participation of middle-aged adults is sought after, but when it comes to the older members of the community, people feel assured of their loyal participation in worship and parish activities. As a result their presence is often enough thought little of: one can be sure of the old! Furthermore, the social threat which the massive rise in the proportion of older people in the overall population of the highly industrialized states has meanwhile come to represent is working its way through to the churches and communities as well. Often enough communities are not pleased at the large number of older members, but find them above all a burden.[3] Even leading figures in pastoral work often express the fear that the presence of too many elderly church members would lead to an even greater distancing of the church from the young, young adults and families, who would not be able to cope with this majority of old people and would not find their own interests and needs sufficiently met.

1. The socialization which has led to the presence of old people in the churches

If we try to explain why so many older people are involved in church life, at present we find two main reasons. First comes the process of socialization to which today's old people were subjected, and secondly the socialization process of old age, which is brought on by specific processes of exclusion.

First, the intensive participation of older people in church and community life, which is evident both in their disproportionately high involvement in Sunday worship[4] and their assent to and trust in the church and their readiness for commitment, is the result of a process of socialization in which religious and social socialization were still largely identical, and religious feeling found its natural expression in intensive church activity. The present generation of old people therefore refutes the unconsidered yet persistently held theory that religion and involvement in the church correlate with old age. Investigations into the psychology of old age show that the notion that it is above all the approach of death which leads old people to intensified religious commitment is untenable.[5]

Secondly, societies which can offer their old members old age only as a 'roleless role' because all the socially significant sectors and functions are by definition reserved for younger people, compel their old people to look for areas which are still open to them. Above all exclusion from professional life, pensioning off, forces on aging people, who are often barely sixty years old, a social disengagement which does not at all (yet) correspond to their personal situation in life, though it is held to be indispensable on economic grounds.[6] It is not surprising that those who have been to such a degree defined and stigmatized as no longer wanted in essential areas of society pay much greater attention to those few areas in which they can still be present. In addition to the leisure sector, these areas include above all the churches (which in social terms are in fact often themselves assigned to the leisure sector). So it is understandable that aging and old people should have special expectations of the churches with their unique situation on the interface of public and private life, expectations of being wanted and accepted, and look for opportunities of participation which have often enough been denied and refused them elsewhere.

II. Understanding from the church and pastoral work with the old

1. The old – a catalyst for the identity of the Christian community

If, then, the organizations and institutions for the old, which are often impressive enough, cannot disguise the fact that older church members nevertheless have unfulfilled wishes and expectations of the church and its communities, the question arises how the communities can in fact do justice to their older members.

Once again we should recall the widespread attitude that too many old people in church are more than younger members can cope with; there is a desire not 'only' for the old but also – perhaps rather – for children, young people and young adults. Behind such a notion there is an understanding of the church community which sees it as exposed and subject to the same laws as those which govern modern businesses: there is a need to fight to make it attractive to the particular groups aimed at, and to do so in the face of hard competition. Those who are sought for as members of the community are not those who have opted for it as a social and religious sphere of life, for whatever individual or social reasons, nor those who live in its area, in a village or suburb. Rather, there is a concern to reach pre-defined groups, and intensive pastoral efforts are made in their direction – though these are seldom crowned with much success. In the face of this understanding of pastoral work in line with the logic of modern economics, it is not surprising that the groups which are particularly sought after generally coincide with the younger and middle-aged age groups for which society generally has a preference.

The most important presupposition for a right and reciprocal relationship between church communities and their older members is therefore an examination of the understanding of the community as such. The question of the attitude of the community to the old is in fact a good catalyst for the identity of a Christian community. In the way in which it lives out *koinonia* between young and old in communication and solidarity, it fulfils itself as a community of Jesus Christ which attempts to follow his standards.

2. *The perception of the old as a multifaceted reality*

Such a self-understanding as community and church comes about through familiarity with the many factors in 'old age' and the development of a perception of the differences in old people's lives.[7] This includes basic knowledge of the social situation of older people at the different stages of their lives. The situation of a fifty-five year old worker with a family who has taken early retirement is not comparable with that of a seventy-five year old former teacher who lives alone, just as the latter is not comparable with a very old occupant of an old people's home in need of nursing care. Without some knowledge of the sociological conditions of aging, of changes in the family cycle, the effects of retirement, the economic situation, conditions at home and leisure activities, education, etc., it is impossible to have a differentiated perception of the lack of homogeneity among the oldest members of the population as a presupposition for differentiated pastoral work with the old. The same goes for the psychological factors of old age. Those who want to support the old in an understanding way, not to mention those who want to offer pastoral help to old people as pastors, need to know about themes of life and how to deal with questions of development at an advanced age; they need to be able to recognize pathological developments which can lead to suicide in old age, and the most frequent geriatric and gerontopsychiatric conditions. Pastors in particular must have some knowledge of religious development in old age, which is sparked off above all by a struggle with life as a whole in the face of advancing death.

Here the ongoing lack of adequate communication of gerontological knowledge within the study of practical theology is disastrous: theologians trained in pastoral work with old people should be in a position to provide basic training and support for the activities of volunteers in the community for their activities in old people's groups and day centres or for dealing with very old church members in the home. If younger people want to help the old to accept and assent to their own life stories and therefore as a result affirm that the last phase of their lives is a meaningful part of life as a whole and so worth living, there is a need for pastoral competence and above all for a climate in the church community which expresses the distinctive dignity of old people and their indispensable charisms for and in the community.

III. Old people and the community – a reciprocal relationship

1. The wisdom of the old
However, those who have asked what old people have to contribute in the communicative process of the church community have recently got into difficulties. Usually a reference is made in a somewhat helpless way to the 'wisdom' of older people, though at the same time this is strangely void of content. Here biblical studies, the psychology of old age and practical theology can help in indicating the specific contribution of older people in terms of wisdom as a virtue of old age.

In essence, wisdom as a biblical virtue, often associated with great age, as the function not merely of long years of life but also of a course of life related to Yahweh and, because of its rarity, valued as a special grace of God, means a life-long search for righteousness which is an expression of the love of God. 'Rich experience is the crown of the aged, and their boast is the fear of the Lord.'

Biblical wisdom in old age defined in this way correlates specifically with the virtue of wisdom in old age which the psychoanalyst E. H. Erikson suggests as the result of a successful solution of the last crisis of maturity in life, the struggle between integrity and despair.[8] Integrity is to be understood as the acceptance and affirmation of one's own unique life, without denying its errors and abysses (in theological terms, guilt) and without succumbing to despair in disgust at it. To integrity corresponds wisdom as 'fulfilled and resolute participation in life in the face of death',[9] which is the expression of hope and faith. In these views Erikson sees himself 'very close to the boundary . . . which separates psychology from ethics'.[10] Though Erikson does not see hope and faith in a specifically Christian sense as hope for the fulfilment of the individual and creation, in faith in Jesus' message of the kingdom of God, it becomes clear that the religious feelings of old age are in a special way an expression of the crisis of the last assent to life which has been overcome in faith. 'The old person is put on the frontier between time and eternity. And there he or she have their most hallowed task. It can be a heavy burden, but God bears it with us . . .'[11] Such religious feelings, which older members of the church community convey to the younger ones in communicative praxis, in the way in which they have lived their lives and particularly in their hope, in the face of the crises over the survival of the human race, for a future for those who come after them, are an indispensable contribution on the part of the old.

2. Old people as tradents of faith

Against this background the question of the old as tradents of faith takes on a new significance, though we must not idealistically ignore the social reality that the old have 'largely lost their role as "bearers of experience" or "mediators of tradition" in today's fast-moving society'.[12] If we are to tackle this situation in a differentiated and critical way, we again need to make clear that the handing down of faith depends on credible tradents and explain why it does. This is not just because faith remains irreplaceably bound up with the possibility of exchanging personal experiences, not least between young and old; the old are particularly important because their own life-long history with God can come to have a special credibility in the eyes of those who still have the greater part of their lives before them. 'The knowledge of faith as practical knowledge . . . also, indeed above all, draws its plausibility from the testimony of successful humanity."[3] 'O God, from my youth you have taught me, and I still proclaim your wondrous deeds' (Ps. 71.17).

3. Learning between the generations

The form and content in which old people can hand on their relevant experiences have in fact changed considerably as a result of developments in society world-wide. There is no longer any interest, say, in their professional knowledge or their patterns of bringing up children. The old people who increasingly find a hearing among the young and young adults are those who are committed to justice, peace and the integrity of creation – they are often regarded as more credible, freer, more ready to repent and more sensitive than members of the middle generation. Integrity and wisdom in old age can express themselves in keeping a community open to the finitude of life, in the face of the ever-present boast of society that 'we can do it'.

Learning between the generations in the context of a community creates the conditions for experiencing community as fellowship, koinonia, between young and old. Following the break-up of the wider family spanning several generations, many children and young people really meet old people only in exceptional situations, like family celebrations. By contrast the community can be a place where it is possible to experience social contacts between the generations which are lacking in everyday life, with the result that negative misconceptions on both sides can be corrected.

Learning between the generations in a perspective orientated on a community also offers the opportunity for different age-groups to work on common questions, like those of more humane forms of housing and lifestyle, social involvement and communication, in a suburb or a town, which does justice to both young and old. Putting one's relevant experiences at the disposal of others in work for a more just human future often finds a ready response among young people.

The aspects developed above indicate that the still predominant practice of conceiving work with the old as a separate sphere of community work, with the danger of ghettoizing the old, needs to be examined. Instead of again subtly excluding old people from the community by creating unnecessary institutions specially for them, it is important so to perceive interests and commitments that they can be carried on in a way which transcends age and sex.

4. The subject option in old age

Against the background of what has been said so far, reciprocity and justice in relations between old people and the community or church are conceivable only if the practical-theological subject option of the old is taken with unconditional seriousness. The worth of old people as subjects needs to be brought out in community praxis. Finally, the basic features of the subject option in old age need to be made specific.

The principle of subsidiarity must also be used in work with the old: as much as possible should be done through old people themselves or at least with them, and as little as possible for them. Reciprocity and equality must be maintained in all circumstances, even in dealing with old people in need of nursing care. This calls above all for sensitivity to the balance between care which is necessary and care which takes over: as much care as necessary, as little as possible. Where in cases of severe illness, a need for nursing care or imminent death nothing more is possible, 'steadfast company'[4] is called for. At all events there is a need to perceive what old people give instead of only seeing what is given to them, or what they once gave and may now expect as 'recompense'.

Learning between the generations calls for attention to the right of the old to be other than we younger ones want them to be, attention to their ways of living, even when they are not our own – indeed precisely then – and particularly their religious forms of expression and their spirituality.

A culture of listening to what the old have to say and of finding a hearing for them where they are not listened to extends into the realm of social and political *diaconia*. The legitimate demands of old people for a dignified old age, which include social safeguards and appropriate participation in society, need to be supported and strengthened. Christian community should not be a 'fellowship of contrast'[5] for old people, which offers them a substitute for the society from which they have been excluded and consoles them for their lack of significance, but a place where there is a plea for a different approach to the old, and by way of anticipation the context of an experiment with an alternative in their own sphere.

Translated by John Bowden

Notes

1. Cf. W. Harenberg (ed.), *Was glauben die Deutschen?*, Munich and Mainz 1968.
2. Cf. M. Blasberg-Kuhnke, Alte`, in C. Bäumler and N. Mette (eds.), *Gemeindepraxis in Grundbegriffen*, Munich and Düsseldorf 1987, 55-63: 57.
3. Ibid., passim.
4. In the Federal Republic more than fifty per cent of Catholics over the age of sixty go to the eucharist every Sunday and a good seventy per cent almost every Sunday. Cf. M. Blasberg-Kuhnke, *Gerontologie und Praktische Theologie*, Düsseldorf 1985, 169ff.
5. Thus already in the 1960s Munnichs could demonstrate empirically that the acceptance of the finitude of one's own life is connected 'among other things with authentic personal religious feelings', whereas religious feelings proved to be a consequence of anxiety over death only in isolated cases. Cf. J. M. A. Munnichs, 'Die Einstellung zur Endlichkeit und zum Tod', in H. Thomae and U. Lehr (ed.), *Altern – Probleme und Tatsachen*, Wiesbaden 1977, 569–612: 608.
6. The disengagement theory, which is one of the most significant sociological theories about aging, essentially says that the withdrawal of the old from society is not only required by society but is also desired by the old themselves and leads to contentment in old age. But this cannot be demonstrated empirically; rather, contentment correlates with the possibility of being able to define the degree of one's participation oneself. Cf. Blasberg-Kuhnke, *Gerontologie* (n. 4), 126–33.
7. Cf. in detail ibid. 15–180.
8. Cf. E. H. Erikson, *Der vollständige Lebenszyklus*, Frankfurt 1988, 78–85.
9. Ibid., 78.
10. Id., *Einsicht und Verantwortung*, Stuttgart 1988, 121.
11. K. Rahner, 'Zum theologischen und anthropologischen Grundverständris des Alters', *Schriften zur Theologie* XV, Zurich–Einsiedeln–Cologne 1983, 315–25: 325.
12. C. Ruback, 'Die Macht der "Alten" stärken. Plädoyer für eine andere Altenarbeit', in B. Kramer (ed.), *Die jungen Alten*, Bonn 1986, 145–62: 151.
13. Blasberg-Kuhnke, *Gerontologie* (n. 4), 263.
14. J. Degen, here cited from N. Mette, 'Gemeinde werden durch Diakonie', in L. Karrer, *Handbuch der praktischen Gemeindearbeit*, Freiburg, Basle and Vienna 1990, 198–214: 207.
15. P. Eicher, 'Kirche als Kontrastgesellschaft?', *Orientierung* 51, 1987, 230–2, attacks an understanding of the church as a contrast society which in the end no longer becomes involved in social conflicts.

III · Cross-Cultural Models for a Social Response to Aging

Religion, Culture and Aging: An Asian Viewpoint

Mary John Mananzan, OSB

I. Introduction

Although aging is a universal phenomenon, the attitudes of society and of the people concerned towards it differ. Two significant factors that account for this difference are belief systems and culture. Aging is a biological, psychological and social process. Because of differences in milieu and world-view, individuals and different groups experience aging in different ways. They experience in dissimilar ways aspects of aging such as life satisfaction, health status and stressful circumstances.

This paper aims to investigate the influence of religion and culture on the attitude of Asian peoples towards aging. It will limit itself to one or two countries of the three main Asian regions: North Asia, South Asia and Southeast Asia.

II. Religion, Culture and Aging in Asia

1. North Asia

Although there are different religions that have prevailed in the different countries of the chopsticks-eating peoples of North Asia, Confucianism is an ethical system originating from the sixth century, when its founder, Confucius, formalized a system of values, of which ancestor worship has become the manifest externalization. This has become inculcated among the Chinese, Japanese, Korean and Thai peoples; so much so that whatever belief system they have, hidden Confucian values will easily show up beneath the surface.

Fundamental to the Confucian philosophy is the idea that a good life depends upon the knowledge and observance of the proper behaviour between one person and another. There are five categories of such interpersonal relationships, namely: 1. parent and child, 2. king and minister, 3. husband and wife, 4. elder sibling and younger sibling, and 5. friend and friend. In practice, the highest respect is given by child to parent, actually to father, since these societies are highly patriarchal. When the parent dies, he or she becomes an object of worship and for three years the child observes ritual mourning. This is the basic relationship, and all the others are merely special applications of it. The most significant festivals aim at the reinforcement of this system, the social matrix of which is the clan.[1]

Filial piety is a high ethical law which Japan shares with the other countries of North Asia. However, this is modified to suit the different structure of the Japanese family. Unlike China and Korea, filial piety is limited to the immediate family, and veneration of ancestors is also limited to grandparents and close relatives. There is also in feudal Japan a strong loyalty to the feudal lord and a sense of belonging to his fief. These values very much affect the attitude of the Japanese towards aging and the aged.[2]

There is a modern Japanese term for middle age – *chunen*, but a pre-modern word *shoro* was used which meant 'beginning of old age'. According to an opinion poll in Japan, this is about the fourth decade of life.[3]

Two traditional 'danger years', *yakudoshi*, that fall during these middle years are widely observed: the thirty-third year for women and the forty-second year for men. During these years, or including the year before or the year after, the Japanese buy amulets and visit shrines for peace of mind or for moments of reflection. Generally, however, middle age is considered by the Japanese as positive. It is considered as the peak period of one's life. It is a time when the person reaches stable status with regard to wealth and authority.

In the case of the woman, middle age marks an official change of status: the transformation of the *yome* (bride or junior wife) to *shutome* (mother-in-law or senior wife). The *shutome* status brings with it the power of being the tutor of the bride apprentice. As the wife of the head of the family, the *shutome* shares his powers, which include economic sanction over the junior couple. Decisions about housekeeping matters are exclusively hers. She prepares the budget, directs the household routines, sets educational policies for grandchildren and even defines the lifestyle of the family members. At least in her own home the *shutome* is considered the family authority on matters of tradition and style, which include family rituals, child rearing and business activities. It has to be noted that the power of the *shutome* is derivative, that is, based on the strength of her relationship with her husband or son. Moreover, there is an implication of an oppression of the *yome*, even if the *shutome* is supposed, ideally, to treat the *yome* with respect and decency.

When the Japanese male reaches the age of sixty, there is a traditional ceremony called the *kanreki iwai*, when he becomes eligible for medicine and social security benefits. However, the present retirement age in business establishments begins as early as fifty-five. Another interim period between retirement and actual old age is thus established. Because of longevity, retirement does not mean the end of employment. It often means the end of one's principal occupation with the possibility of a job shift. But since permanent employment after retirement is not possible, this job shift is accompanied by loss of income and very often by an emotional sense of loss. This is because of the already-mentioned Confucian value of belongingness to the fief. In modern times this loyalty is to the company. Douglas Sparks explains:

> If one asks a skilled American worker what he does for a living, he might answer that he is, say, a welder. His Japanese counterpart, on the other hand, would be more likely to answer with the name of his company, without reference to this job classification: 'a Mitsubishi man' or 'a Sony employee', for example. The American is more apt to think of his work in self-referent terms (what I do); the Japanese worker, blue collar or white, will probably consider his group affiliation (his company, where we work) more important than his current task assignment.[4]

Thus for the Japanese employee to leave a company where he has spent most of his adult life can cause anxiety, role dislocation and a sense of isolation. In fact this, more than age, is what determines the perception of the onset of aging.

When finally reaching actual old age, the Japanese has the distinct advantage, shared with the other Confucian-influenced countries, that the elderly is traditionally and ideally the recipient of filial piety and is freed from responsibilities and constraints, living among his descendants and supported by the oldest son. Especially in rural Japan, the elderly are held as exemplary figures who deserve respect by virtue of age. In modern urban Japan, however, as in the other countries, there may be an erosion of this value.

2. South Asia

The representative country for this region is India, the second largest country in the world and home of great religious traditions. Hinduism is the major religion, about eighty-three per cent of its population being believers. About twelve per cent are Muslims and three per cent

Christians, with the exception of the state of Kerala, which has about thirty-five per cent Christians.

The Hindu philosophy rests on three basic concepts: Karma, Dharma and Rebirth. It is difficult to discuss these concepts in a few lines, but here is a simple explanation:

> *Kharma*: one is born when one deserves to be, based on one's previous life. *Dharma*: one does one's duty well within the state of life where one is born, never trying to move out of caste, but accepting any inconveniences. *Rebirth*: if one follows Kharma and Dharma, one will reach Mukti (union with God) or be reborn into a higher caste in the next life. If one lives a bad life, rebirth may be to a lower caste, or outside human life as animal or insect.[5]

The Indian family was and still is based on an extended or joint family system, which originated in Vedic times. A close link was maintained between siblings, uncles and aunts, cousins and nephews and grandparents, who lived usually under the same roof or group of roofs and who owned the immovable property of the line communally. It is both patriarchal and patrilineal. The oldest male member is absolute head. Members are related by an interlocking pattern of mutual dependence, the individual being subordinate to the collective group and the younger generation being strictly controlled by the elders.

As in the countries of North Asia, there are family ceremonies venerating the ancestors. One is known as the *stradda*, at which balls of rice called *pinda* are offered. Sons, grandsons and great-grandsons of the deceased join the ceremony, and it is believed that three generations of the dead participate in its benefits. Thus in linking the living and the dead, this ceremony becomes a potent force in consolidating the family.

The life-span of the Indian[6] covers roughly four stages, according to the Aryan tradition which is described by A. L. Basham:

> Just as Aryan society was divided into four classes, so the life of the individual Aryan was divided into four stages: his investiture with the sacred thread, when he put his childhood behind him . . . leading a celibate and austere life as a student at the home of his teacher; next, having mastered Vedas . . . he returned to his parental home, and was married, becoming a householder . . . when, well advanced in middle age, he had seen his children's children and had thus surely established his line, he left his home for the forest to become a hermit . . . by meditation and penance he freed his soul from material things, until at last, a very old man, he left his hermitage and became a homeless wanderer with all his earthly ties broken.[7]

Although this scheme represents the ideal rather than the real, nevertheless it could serve as a framework round which the life of the individual could be modelled. Here the focus is on the fourth stage. According to the letter of the Sacred Law, when a householder's hair turns white, and he has seen his sons' children, he should become a forest hermit. Before his death, he should become a wanderer. In reality only a small proportion of the elderly men followed this scheme strictly. Most of them, however, still take up asceticism in their old age in a hut in the family compound or a secluded room in their old home.

Many factors affect the perception of aging. In India, the closeness of the family which enables the elderly persons to live in the bosom of their family is a positive factor in giving a feeling of security to the elderly. They catch up with the local news from their peers whom they meet daily at the open field which serves as a communal toilet. Personal fulfilment also depends on the feeling of usefulness to the family or community. Being able to care for grandchildren gives this sense of usefulness, especially to elderly women. The special importance of the *guru* in Indian society also contributes to the sense of personal fulfilment among the elderly, who are looked up to as teachers and authorities on sacred tradition.

Here, as in the case of Japanese society, a special discussion of elderly women is called for. Indian widows face a sad situation. In general, a widow could not remarry. This rule was not, of course, strictly kept. But in families which adhered to the letter of the law the lot of the widow was very hard. She remained with her in-laws and family and it was their responsibility to look after her. She lived as an ascetic sleeping on hard ground, eating only a simple meal a day, wearing no coloured garments. Most shaved their heads. The widow had to maintain this austere regimen in the home so that she would remarry her former husband in the next life. Any breach of her ascetic discipline could mean an unhappy rebirth for herself and endanger her husband, who might suffer for her shortcomings. Wherever she went her presence cast a shadow of sadness. She was not allowed to attend family festivals for fear of bringing bad luck. She could not return to her parents but was shunned even by servants. No wonder women preferred the self-immolation of *sati*, joining their husbands in the funeral pyre rather than living such a miserable life.

The majority of old people in India accept death as a natural progression of age. This acceptance of death contributes to the relative serenity of the aged. However there could be some anxiety over funeral rites, because for the Hindu safe passage to the next world depends on certain rituals in cremation and the *srada* ceremonies. Many put money aside and women keep jewellery to be sold for their funerals.

3. Southeast Asia

Most of the peoples of Southeast Asia are essentially of a Malay stock. Islam and Christianity are the major religions that have gained a foothold in this region. However, there is an underlying belief system that is a combination of ancestor and nature worship which has been designated as animism, a term that has acquired a deprecatory nuance.

A recent study (1987) by Heather Strange in two rural Malay villages provides an insight into the attitude on aging among the Malays.

Malaysia's population is young, with about forty-one per cent under fifteen years of age. People in their fifties are considered old, and the curious thing is that in rural areas they tend to add years to their official ages, thus placing themselves in the category of the elderly or the *orangtua*. A reason for this age exaggeration in a predominantly Muslim community may be because elders might be learned in Islam, wealthy, or fill other statuses that merit respect. They are considered more knowledgeable about family and customary matters (*adat*) than younger persons and therefore may be considered wise in the family context.[8]

The average Malay elder is treated with respect and politeness by members of the community, both in polite forms of words and body language. The status 'elder' allows a person to avoid activities, commitments or responsibilities without being subjected to sanctions. For a woman there is a relaxation of many modesty rules imposed on younger women. Older women can joke with men and relax on their porches in full view of anyone, dressed only in a sarong cinched under the armpits.

Support for destitute parents is required both by custom and by Muslim law. The prestige of parents grows in proportion to their children's generosity. There is no implication that this acceptance of assistance detracts from their atuonomy as people.[9] One argument for having a large family in rural Malay is this expectation of support in one's old age.

As in other societies, widows tend to be disadvantaged. Given widows and widowers who are elders, the widower will likely marry a younger woman within a year of his wife's death, while the widow will either not have the opportunity or most often will not choose to do so. Since few women own productive land, they must live in somebody else's house, usually in one of their children's houses.

The data in Strange's study about the criteria for the Malay's worry or lack of worry over future old age are significant. The computerized data show that those who say they have no or little worry about their old age:

Have one or more child living in the village, especially if the child is a daughter.
Have one or more grandchildren of either sex living nearby.

Say that they give assistance in some way to children or grandchildren.

Receive regular visits from children and grandchildren and receive help from them.

Characterize neighbours as helpful and themselves as helpful to neighbours.

Own the home they are living in.

Have had no recent illness.

Depict the village as a good place to live in.

Think developments such as good roads, schools and other improvements desirable.[10]

The same variables would hold good for the elderly in another country in Southeast Asia, the Philippines, whose people are basically of Malay stock.

Like Malaysia, the Philippines has a predominantly young population. In contrast to Malaysia, the predominant religion is Christianity, eighty-five per cent of the population being Catholics and six per cent Protestants, and only four per cent Muslims. A similar kinship system exists, with the same emphasis on family closeness and interdependence.

With regard to attitudes toward aging, there are many similarities: members of the older generation, as in Malaysia, expect respect from the younger generation. Age is likewise a factor in establishing status, together with a good grasp of local lore and traditional practices and healing abilities.

F. Landa Jocano summarizes the corollaries of the Filipinos' equation of age with wisdom and experience:

1. All younger members of the group should respect the older ones.
2. In social gatherings, the older members should be listened to and their authority acknowledged.
3. Age has the wisdom of experience; youth has the immaturity of impulsive action and the rashness of innocence.
4. The judgment of the young may be right but is seldom wise.
5. While age is wisdom, it must be coupled with dignity and knowledge of traditions and customs.
6. Supernatural sanctions support the wisdom of age; a curse from an older man activates supernatural powers to impose corresponding punishments.[11]

In a study made on aging among Filipinos, fifty-five per cent answered the question whether they wanted to grow old in the affirmative and the reason as a philosphical acceptance of the inevitable. Some cited as their reason the desire to guide their children and see grandchildren; to enjoy life and the fruit of their labour. Those who answered in the negative, gave reasons such as 'I do not like to be ugly, weak.' 'It is difficult to live old.' 'I do not like my children to be burdened in taking care of me.'

With regard to the feelings and attitudes of younger Filipinos to the elderly, the study finds that the present generation still has an impressive level of love and respect for old people, even those who are outside one's family. There seems to be less fear of old people, especially in urban settings, which is taken as a sign of more open and informal relations with the elderly. But this may also mean a decline in the authority wielded by senior members of the family over the youth. There is a general agreement that parents should be cared for and served more particularly in their old age. It is not unusual for old people who have no relatives to be taken care of by neighbours and other people unrelated to them, for it is generally believed that helping unfortunates, especially the aged, usually brings blessings (*suerte*) . . . However, there is a consensus that certain traditional signs of respect, such as kissing the hand, are no longer appropriate.

There is a tendency of Filipinos to become more religious as they grow old. They find consolation in the Christian belief that human life is a pilgrimage to God the Father and old age is the final stage of this journey. Living as pilgrims, they gradually detach themselves from things. An old Filipino Dominican is quoted as having answered the question 'How old are you?' with 'One day nearer to eternal life'.

The following conclusion is true in the societies of Southeast Asia:

> The family is still, and even in the future, the major support of the elderly. Informal community support is readily available where blood relation exists and adherence to traditions is still strong. Commitment to an institution is still an unthinkable option for elderly care in the rural areas.[12]

III. Conclusion

From the foregoing study of aging in the context of Asian religions and cultures, one observation that could be made is that in spite of the different religions and varying cultural practices found in different Asian countries, one common feature stands out: the emphasis on the family. The extension of the family differs from country to country, but the same value of interdependence and loyalty is observed within the respective group. This gives a person a certain rootedness and a sense of belonging, which accounts for the emotional security and serenity of Asians in their old age in spite of undergoing unsettling changes in their lives.

In Asia, we have also seen an emphasis on traditional values, practices and rituals. The elderly are seen as the repository of this wisdom, which gives them a special role and status in their old age with a corresponding sense of usefulness. There is thus a positive attitude towards aging. The prevailing ancestor worship which underlies the different religions in Asia likewise assures an attitude of reverence and respect for the old.

The generally non-materialistic attitude of Asians towards life gives them a certain person-orientedness which is contrasted with the object-and-goal orientation of many Western peoples. Thus it is unthinkable for Orientals, no matter how busy they are, to leave a dying relative unattended. Filipino nurses who have become overseas workers in the West relate their shock and dismay at the practice in Western hospitals of leaving dying patients alone. Old people in Asia are assured that members of their families and friends will surround them at their death bed and will help them in their last existential experience.

Religions, whatever they are, tend to give believers a positive attitude towards death; it is seen by Buddhists as a passage to Nirvana; by Hindus as the possibility of rebirth to a higher caste; by Christians as the joining of the spirit world. This view somehow enables old people to accept their death with serenity and peace, and even with expectation and hope.

Not everything is quite without problems in the matter of aging in the Asian context. There are the inevitable frictions when different generations live closely with one another. As was also shown, gender analysis would point to certain disadvantages to older women, especially widows, not suffered by elderly men. There might be advantages of better care in institutions that cannot be given in home care of the elderly. Industrialization and urbanization among the newly-industrialized countries of Asia pose new problems of erosion of traditional values and practices as does the limitation of living space in modern urban homes, which may not allow room for grandparents.

The challenge for Asian peoples is to combine in a creative way the technological advances and traditional values with a system of modern care for the aged that could assure them of effective support and provide them with the new conveniences that could make them spend their twilight years in ease, comfort and a sense of fulfilment.

Notes

1. C. Osgood, *The Koreans and Their Culture*, Tokyo 1954, 38–9.
2. Cf. R. Benedict, *The Chrysanthemum and the Sword*, New York 1946.
3. Kobe Shimbun Sha, in D. Plath, *Adult Episodes in Japan*, Leiden 1975, 52.
4. D. Parks, 'The Still Rebirth', in Plath, *Adult Episodes* (n. 3), 65.
5. A Merriman, 'Social Customs Affecting the Elderly Women in Indian Society', in D. Bromley (ed.), *Gerontology: Social and Behavioural Perspectives*, London 1984, 156.

6. A. L. Basham, *The Wonder That Was India*, New York 1968, 155.

7. Ibid., 158.

8. H. Strange, 'Rural Malay Aged', in *Aging and Cultural Diversity*, Massachusetts 1987, 21–2.

9. Ibid., 24.

10. Ibid., 32.

11. F. L. Jocano, 'Elements of Filipino Social Organization', in Yasuchi Kikuchi, *Philippine Kinship and Society*, Quezon City 1989, 22–3.

12. UST, Social Resource Centre, pp. 152–3.

Religion, Culture and Aging: A Latin American Viewpoint

Ivone Gebara

In a continent in which infant mortality reaches impressive proportions, especially in the poorest areas, discussing the ethical aspects of aging may seem a marginal topic.

In Latin America the primordial question is still that of the survival of thousands of children who don't manage to reach the age of five. This is still the great moral issue in a continent marked by a history of conquest, colonization and exploitation which has taken different forms and has always continued to marginalize the masses, the great majority of whom are denied access to a decent life.

Nevertheless, despite early death, and flagrant disrespect for the right to life in all its manifestations, aging is a painful reality for much of the Latin American population. Its features are for the most part different from those it assumes in Western societies, where we are currently witnessing a great increase in the elderly population to the extent that the phenomenon of longevity is coming to be considered as a growing challenge to the various sectors of society. Issues such as euthanasia are still not priorities in Latin American ethical studies as they are in other continents.

My discussion, though rooted in Latin America, does not presume to encompass the phenomenon of aging in the cultural diversity of the continent. I am not presenting statistics or forecasts of the proportion of elderly in the population. I offer to the public some personal reflections and intuitions from the point of view of theological anthropology, the product of contact with a number of elderly people from different places and social classes, especially women, for whom 'aging' seems to be a special experience, to some extent different from 'aging' in men.

This article has three sections.

1. Wrinkles: furrows opened in body and soul;

2. The immorality of social behaviours in relation to aging;
3. The role of religion in human aging: some aspects.

1. Wrinkles: furrows opened in body and soul

Life continually leaves its marks on the body, traces firm lines which follow the contours of the face, opening up furrows, like indelible signs which multiply and become bolder over the years. It gradually whitens and thins hair, and makes the body feel the inexorable passing of the years.

Life writes our history on our very bodies, on our gestures, on our eyes. The journeys we have made, the years we have lived, the joys and sorrows, the hopes, the hidden desires, all seem to converge on this body, which can now disclose a story, let the wrinkles speak, because of course they have a story. The face of age is history, allows an interpretation, provokes interpretations, makes one think.

To age is to notice this passing of life, constant and intense, as though we could look in a mirror and, in one minute, see the transformation of the same face passing through all its stages before our very eyes, gradually changing from young to old.

Aging, while a constant for human beings, is not a homogeneous process, but variable and with its own place in different cultures, periods and social classes.

Sometimes I'm tempted to think that there is a 'destiny' which marks the aging process in certain lives. It is as though from infancy or childhood you can already see the type of old age which is to come. In most cases it's impossible to escape this 'destiny'. Society imposes it like a sentence to be served to the end of one's days. It is in this sense that aging is a multiple phenomenon on the Latin American continent because of its huge contrasts, above all those caused by the inequality of social and economic conditions. For example, there are old men and women in the various countries of Latin America who live as though they were in the First World, that is, have the material conditions which allow them to age with dignity.

This is really the First World within the Third World, living consciously or unconsciously at the expense of the latter. I'm not going to talk about that, because in a way what is said about aging as a challenge in the West is almost totally applicable to this minority who are born in comfort and age in comfort, apart from the intrinsic problems of this age group. In Latin America, too, within the middle and upper classes, its numbers are increasing and challenge the statistics which show the increasing longevity of these minorities on the continent.

Under the first heading I shall concentrate on aging among the poor, especially among women, who often die old before their time, exhausted by work and hard living conditions. They say that in the Middle Ages the average age of death in Western Europe was between forty and fifty. The same holds good today in the poor populations of Latin America. At this age or before the poor lose their teeth, their sight begins to fail, the diseases of old age come early, their bodies lose their tone, and they live in their bodies the life expectancies of past centuries.

My thoughts turn first to the women of the countryside, those whose births mingled with the birth of the ears of corn and of the animals. I remember familiar faces, some very dear, which quickly took on the same 'fate' as the plants, entered into the same cycle of fertility as the land, faces which grew and reproduced, were burnt by heat and cold, and whole bodies marked by deep wrinkles which sometimes turned into folds of fallen skin hanging from the body. These women never used moisturizing creams or any sort of cosmetics. They never had any plastic surgery or consulted beauticians about avoiding the effects of aging. They fell asleep, finally mingling with the earth, joining the natural cycle of the things of nature.

I now look at those who, while still young, left the country, 'their land', and came to grow old as domestics in the cities, looking for the daily bread of survival. Some became trusted nurses, exploited, perhaps with affection; others became prostitutes, loved, lovers, welcomed or rejected. Some perhaps retain from their lives the sweet memory of work-worn arms, welcoming and untiring, or the memory of the wonderful stories which filled many of their childhoods, stories told especially at night in those special hours when sleep is about to come to the children. However, most of these women have vanished from history and from the memories of those they served, because in general the lives of the impoverished masses leave hardly a trace and go to swell the anonymous mass of history.

For the great majority of Latin American women, trapped in poverty, aging means living, but with reduced strength, the lives they have always lived; that is, the daily domestic struggle to survive but with the additional problems of disease, undernourishment, dependence, sometimes abandonment, the almost total absence of assistance from the public authorities. Those who reach old age, not as many as in the First World, suffer most in the big cities, from the grief of being considered a burden, a part of society which doesn't produce, but only consumes.

In fact, however, if we look beyond the definitions fixed by capitalist society, definitions based on productivity, we will find that many elderly women are still 'heads' of families, look after grandchildren, go out to work, especially when parents or the mother have left the children to look for work or for some other reason. They are the old educators, who, to the best of their abilities and with all their limitations, maintain a minimum of psychological, emotional and family stability for thousands of children and young people with no opportunity to enjoy the company of their mothers and fathers.

A woman's life-span seems to be longer than a man's. This is an observable fact of life which I shall not try to analyse. I simply note it to make the point that for many women a long life can be a 'cross'. This is reflected in the countless difficulties of everyday life and the constant effort to find a positive meaning in life as an alternative to the one imposed by society.

Instead of valuing the wisdom and work of elderly women, Latin American society makes them free domestic labour. It perpetuates the exploitation of women, but adds to it a further element in the spiral of exploitation in capitalist societies, namely exploitation in the form of disrespect for old people.

Growing old in Latin America means being continually confronted with the 'young values' thrust on the whole population by the media. The dominant culture demands that everyone should adapt to its values, which are based on consumerism and directed towards profit. Because of their situation poor women have no access to so-called 'young values': to young fashions, to young people's sports, to bodies modelled on those of young women. In old age these women are often objects of laughter and jokes as a sort of culturally backward and physically unfit 'race'.

What is serious about this situation is that the standard established and propagated by the media is accepted as the last word on human nature. The majority of the population lack the critical distance and the education which would enable them to create alternatives which would show more respect for life.

There can be no doubt that the idolatry of youth conceals a lack of a sense of meaning in human existence as a whole, in its unity and connectedness, and a failure in the interpretation and understanding of its different stages. This idolatry hits the elderly hardest because they no longer see themselves as persons whose value is recognized, and it tends to create in many of them an attitude of conformism or increasing distress as their lives seem ever more forgotten and useless. Elderly women often feel a sharp break between themselves and younger generations, especially when confronted with media which present them with a world which is increasingly different from that of their everyday lives. For the great majority television and radio merely provide a 'diversion', to enable them not to think about the real nature of their lives. Television also enables them to 'see other women', those who are young, who have money, vitality and energy.

Television reminds them that their time is over: they are no longer needed, no longer talked about.

It is clear that there is a sort of violence practised against elderly women. They absorb the values purveyed by the surrounding society and enter into a process of rejecting their own selves, a process expressed in a rejection of the body and sex or in an acceptance which reinforces still more the process of alienating aging.

Growing old in Latin America means carrying with one wrinkles like open furrows in the body and the soul, wrinkles produced by time, suffering and the poverty imposed by a system which has not yet had its fill of human blood, despite so many predictions of its imminent death.

This aging which is unworthy of human beings brings us to the heart of the moral questions.

2. The immorality of social behiavours in relation to aging

A general abstract discussion of the morality of various forms of behaviour could lead us into a variety of digressions which never got down to real issues. However, a discussion of morality has to be fleshed out in a description of forms of behaviour, relationships, proposals, individual and collective visions and predictions, influenced by the whole range of historical and cultural factors and situations. These rest on a foundation which is essential to all creatures, that is, the inalienable right to life, understood here in its various manifestations, the co-existence of its different forms, in respect for the autonomy and integrity of the different creatures. Accordingly, when we talk about the morality of forms of social behaviour we are talking at the same time about a way of understanding human life and living creatures in general as worthy of absolute value, supreme value. In other words, to talk about the morality of forms of behaviour means discussing a sort of historic human 'universal' capable of guaranteeing a just and respectful co-existence between all individuals, within their different cultures and groups. This historical 'universal' is always marked by the limitations of our judgments, our intentions, our individual and collective interests. Of course, we describe it as being beyond all those factors, but in the detail of our actions this 'universal', this 'golden rule' for all human behaviour, is always conditioned by all the vicissitudes and limitations of our existence. As a result, there is a collective responsibility incumbent on all of us to preserve this 'universal' so that it may continue to underpin the continually renewed search for relations of justice and respect in all human societies.

If we turn to the specific question of aging, we know, for example, that there have been peoples who ate their old, either when they were found to be of no more use to society or in an attempt to assimilate their qualities. Other peoples revered their elders and gave them important tasks as leaders and advisers (gerontocracy). Others again stressed the wisdom and peace of old age as guarantees for the continuing existence of the social group. There have been diverse attitudes and forms of behaviour towards old age, and it is always our own understanding of what is moral which governs our judgment as to whether or not certain types of behaviour were or are to be considered moral. That is why it is important for us to realize how the choice and experience of our own values conditions our understanding and judgment of the morality of different types of behaviour, even if we make the effort to respect the usages, customs and traditions of different cultures.

In Latin America to discuss the moral problem of aging is to open the old sore which disfigures society as a whole, the lack of decent living conditions for the great majority of the population. Old men and women form part of this throng of the forgotten, who keep on having to listen to empty promises of future prosperity which will finally pull them out of their poverty.

The maintenance of this age-old situation is a sign of a society built on immoral foundations. It is a society built on a real, historical belief in fundamental inequality between individuals, despite the paeans in every country to fundamental equality and inalienable rights. Starting from this paradoxical and unjust situation, this lack of respect, we can identify some current forms of behaviour towards elderly people, and this will give us a better understanding of the moral issues involved in aging in Latin America.

One problem of which there is little awareness is that of the imposition of patterns of behaviour on old men and women, to some degree independently of their membership of a particular social class. Irrespective of their class, these people belong to a particular category: the elderly, those who are preparing to leave the stage of history, those who have retired from active involvement in the world of remunerated labour, who are withdrawing from politics and the whole range of great decisions. Elderly men and women in general assimilate these patterns, make them their own, reinterpret them in terms of their individual and social history, and most finally come to accept that they are 'no use', and that the only right they have is to while away the time.

Refusal to follow the established patterns is regarded as abnormal behaviour. Surprise, shock and even criticism are the reactions when men and women try to find alternatives, adopt other types of behaviour, step out of line.

An old person is supposed to be kindly, mustn't complain, mustn't want things, mustn't make demands, except those admitted by the established patterns. Old people are supposed to be submissive, caring, affectionate, to obey their children or the 'adults' who guide and support them. They must be wise, patient and calm, and not hold what are called 'extreme' views.

Their right to exist is guaranteed by obedience to the established norms, by their unquestioning submission to the rules of the 'adult game'. In this way culture constructs a sort of prison in which all are held bound by thick ropes, but in most cases the ropes are felt and experienced as part of the nature of things, of what is normal, part of life.

To the extent that the elderly flee from the prison of social acceptability, they are called 'unusual', 'crazy', 'confused'. Their allotted place is restricted to that fixed by society and culture, which seem to insist on erecting rigid barriers between the different stages of human life. Acceptance of plurality where old people are concerned is increasingly remote in our so-called pluralistic society. Its pluralism in fact is also limited to certain models; it is a pluralism which is rigid, predetermined, which excludes much and is deeply anti-democratic.

Such vehemently affirmed ideals as personal independence, freedom of choice, the right to display desire, physical, sexual and intellectual energy, democratic participation and a share in responsibility are considered not only as 'normal', but also as 'essential' to life in societies which claim to be democratic. However, when elderly people try to fulfil these ideals, barriers are erected, and in the name of care for the elderly they are deprived of even the desire to live and to continue to make their contribution to the best of their ability. When old age arrives, the values so loudly proclaimed by society seem to evaporate; democratic rights seem to be withdrawn and in their place submission and obedience to new rules become the order of the day.

There are no social choices in aging; there is a 'destiny' which in most cases is predetermined and cannot be evaded, especially when a person is poor and has lived all his or her life without choice, at least in social terms. An alternative, more just social order is difficult to imagine in a society in which fewer and fewer people have the chance of a dignified, creative and pleasurable life. Exclusion appears the best solution, and the easiest: exclusion encouraging good feelings, respect and pity for the poor dears. Respect and pity may in part conceal the diabolical aims of a society led by the forces of death, a society almost bereft of human purpose but wearing a mask of humanism. 'Corrupting reverence' eventually becomes intoxicating, and gradually takes on moral weight as it is accepted by those who are sensitive to certain sorts of language, and by the elderly. The elderly, too, begin to feel themselves to be objects of pity and respect; they start to pity themselves, and as the self-pity increases, so does the alienation, the need for protection, the regression which can reach the stage of total dependence. They are excluded from the 'normal' everyday life of citizens, and limited to their homes or the few institutions which offer shelter to the elderly. Tomorrow is no longer, for most of them, an event to be looked forward to, which could be full of pleasant surprises, a new possibility, but the days are counted, 'one more day' in which we are closer to death, more useless, more in need of pity. Dignity is reduced as physical powers ebb in the 'wonderful world' of 'young values' propagated with such force by capitalist societies.

This raises a question of fundamental importance for Latin America, that of the introjection of marginal status and, as a result, the creation of an individual and collective sense of being less, of being unworthy, of not being like those who know, who have, who are strong. The dominant culture excludes so much that it makes people believe that it is impossible to change the present situation, and the absence of this sort of hope reinforces the *status quo* desired by those who hold power. The moral issue here lies in the fact that the elderly, who are, unknown to themselves, part of the marginal culture of the masses, construct within themselves, under the pressure of social forces, a reduced image, an image of dependent beings, forced to the end of the their days to beg for the right to exist with a minimum of dignity. Being nothing more than an old man or an old woman can mean doubting whether one is still completely human. This doubt is absorbed as a result of a subtle imposition by society, which, despite its humanist language, excludes from its humanism individuals who get in the way or whom it regards as a threat. Humanist language becomes demagogy in the service of the interests of minorities thirsty for power and profit.

Why is there this fear of elderly people? Elderly people are indeed threatening to a society in which the ideals of youth, productivity, consumption and intense mobility are the most important. Old age is threatening becuase it is a reminder of something else, a reminder of where we are all going; old age forces us to face our personal future, strikes at the desire for eternal youth, brings up the idea of death as the inevitable dusk waiting for us all. The much-vaunted 'wisdom' of the elderly is useless or, better, its use is to be romantic talk without practical value. It is no longer able to join the frenetic rhythm of our socities, especially in the big cities.

The avalanche of new discoveries, new information, new methods and different customs increasingly makes it impossible for elderly people to gain access to the insatiable quest for novelty. Now the old start to learn from the young, whose condition makes them better able to tap the innovations of modern technology. The old depend on the instant wisdom of the young to keep more or less up-to-date.

We find that older people, with a few exceptions, accept this marginaliz-ation in the face of the difficulty of keeping up with the dizzying rhythm of modern society. Very quickly they are 'out of it', and being 'out of it' both marginalizes them and makes them a threat. The threat comes from their message that soon we, too, the adults of now, those who are now in charge, will be 'out of it'; we, too, will be experiencing the marginalization we are now conniving at. Pushing this marginalization away from us, denying its existence, talking only about youth and old people being 'young at heart', is thus a way of exorcizing the fear of aging, of feeling that our bodies are no longer keeping up with the 'official rhythm'.

For those who are 'rich in years', a different human rhythm is necessary, one which could be quite easily accepted if the values of our societies were not so dominated by the profit which finally becomes a force that destroys human life as a continuum.

As Simone de Beauvoir puts it very well, the dehumanizing effect of old age is nothing separate from the totality of what happens in our society. As a result, 'to demand that men (and women) should remain men (and women) during their final years of life implies radical change. It is impossible to secure this result through a few limited reforms which leave the system intact: the exploitation of workers, the fragmentation of society, the poverty of a culture reserved to a caste of mandarins are what produce as their consequence inhuman old age.'[1]

3. The role of religion in human aging: some aspects

The great religions have always had the important role of drawing attention to dimensions of life which we frequently forget or undervalue. Their mission, in other words, is to awaken 'stony hearts' to care for 'the poor, the widow, the orphan and the stranger', to help in raising up marginalized and abandoned groups. They try to feel their way towards, and answer, the question of the ultimate meaning of existence and of the individual.

In connection with aging, we need only remember, for example, the Buddha in his famous meeting with the old man as he left his father's castle. That meeting made him think about the meaning of human existence and shaped the rest of his life. We should also remember the various institutions which have originated within Christianity to shelter and care for the elderly. Whole lives have been devoted to this social enterprise, which was identified with consecration to God and his service.

The way the old are treated in the different religions seems paradoxical if we compare it with the actions of contemporary consumer societies, especially in the Western world. While these societies seem to forget the elderly and even strip them of any guarantee of a dignified life, the religions attempt to devise meaningful ethical behaviour patterns, even if in many places their social impact is less than in the past.

In Latin America, while the media still propagate what they call youth values, as it were expelling old age from 'official' human society, there are still oases of traditional religious culture which form the basis of what might be called a 'theology of old age'. This theology is based on particular popular attitudes, current especially among the poor majority in rural areas, which convey a belief that God is concealed in a special way in old people. To deny food and shelter to the elderly is thus to deny them to God himself. A hungry old person is as shocking as a hungry child, and often much more dramatic in that such old people represent a life ending in poverty and abandonment, without any real chance of future recovery and so with no practical hope of change. A life which has already had more than its share of suffering ends in the agonizing experience of the human condition gradually diminishing until the last breath.

There is a moral system in this popular theology of old age. It is as though the presence of the old were an appeal to us to adopt certain forms of behaviour. In them we see our own future. There is frequently a conscious or unconscious near-identification, so strong that it is impossible to say whether we love the old person for his or her own sake or for our own. As a result there is something like a popular moral-religious attitude in which my neighbour (the old woman/man), God and I are all closely bound together. The poor do not put this attitude into these formal theological terms, but they live the experience at a deep level.

The poor often see themselves in needy old people, themselves as they would be if totally abandoned: human beings dependent on others for help, shelter, daily bread and affection.

In this situation 'loving others as oneself' seems to take on an important physical and historical reality, even if in most cases these attitudes lack a collective political dimension and a critical analysis of what causes the inhuman conditions of old age. It is the immediate that counts, and in this perspective the figure of the old man or woman is a moral challenge, as though God were hidden in them waiting for a welcoming response.

In the popular imagination God is envisaged as an old man with long white hair and a long white beard, and a face both tender and demanding. God's old age seems to be a symbol of old age as human 'destiny', the final recognition in God of our own human face at the end of its historical journey. It should be noted that in this popular conception God doesn't grow old. God is imagined as being old, as though old age were a sort of divine attribute, an eternal state or situation of God, as if the final end of the human state present in old age were fixed permanently in God. This 'projection' seems to point to a sort of popular wisdom which reveals an impressive synchrony between God, the world and humanity. There is a saying that 'God is older than the world', but to call something old is to apply a human characteristic, to use a human word which describes oneself. And, indeed, this word is used of the God with a human face. God's old age embodies his eternity, his wisdom, his infinite mercy and our desire that he should be all this. In the 'imagined' face of the old God all old men and women want to encounter, as it were, their ultimate truth.

It may be true that this anthropomorphic image conjures up the old patriarch, the master and paterfamilias, a dominant figure in Latin American culture since colonial times, but it needs to be said that in the popular imagination this old person with no doubt masculine features is beyond questions of sexism. This person is a sort of 'icon' in which the whole human condition can be symbolically contained, an 'icon' which anticipates human destiny and makes God take it on himself. In this 'icon' maternal or paternal features, elements of compassion and tenderness, and of the end of human life, mingle, just as everything is jumbled together in human life.

In devaluing old age, in rejecting this part of their own selves, the iconoclasts of our societies open up a gulf within human nature itself, make it rebel against itself and abandon the totality of the unified evolutionary process which makes us what we are. The exclusive behaviour which characterizes modern societies alienates us from a part of ourselves, leads us to deny it as something ugly, shameful and worthless. This part of us is the human state in old age, continually denied despite its presence and insistently camouflaged to make us forget our end, our future.

Modern societies seem to want a future confined within their own models of the present and seek to impose types of behaviour on elderly people who resist the popular culture. There is clearly something here which contradicts the tenets of religions and the riches of the popular imagination. There is a disguised anti-humanism which takes on frightening proportions: the elimination of old people and the elimination of the human face of the 'old God' go more or less hand in hand.

The 'old God' has become a figure of fun, a cultural archaism, religious prehistory. While this may be true in the critical terms of anthropology and theology, it nevertheless contains serious implications to which Western theology, even in the Third World, has not paid sufficient attention.

We talk and write a lot about the demands of the God of life, the God of the prophets, of Jesus, of Mary, the God of the poor, but our new talk about God seems not to give the experience of old age its proper place. This is a God who invites us to the just battle for liberation, the effective practice of justice, but there is something missing from this battle. The something is perhaps an empy space, where we have not found room for the glowing and yet withered faces of those who seem to be outside the battle waged by young people and adults, the battle for liberation. We have not found room for the faces of those who, because of their age, are 'led' by others and perhaps are going where they would rather not go. I admit that I have difficulty in expressing this intuition or perception. It is as though we, too, in the domain of religious experience, regarded old people as retaining the original content of their faith, as if they were not allowed to experience something else or to express their deep experiences; as if we listened to them talking about God and found what we heard merely charming, as we describe details of our long past childhood as charming. Perhaps unconsciously we don't want to know what old people have to say about God. We don't want them to 'produce' him, nor do we want to help them in this type of 'production'. It is probable that what they have to say terrorizes and threatens us.

What we feel is the existence of a gulf between the religious experience of the elderly and that of young or middle-aged adults. If this feeling is an inevitable fact, in part the product of our times and a result of the human condition, it is at the same time an invitation to humanity, to engage in a serious dialogue with itself, since this humanity expresses within itself the divine.

I do not want to fall into crude anthropomorphisms, but there is something we need to preserve in elderly people's experience of God. It is not just regression to the God of childhood, but a growth pointing to 'something more' than the kind old man with a white beard, pointing to the need to define a meaning for the human condition as a whole, a meaning which brings hope, is able to help us discover the positive side of aging, of 'returning' to the earth, of mingling with the dust of the roads, of being manure, seed, flower, fruit, food, which continues in the extraordinary and mysterious adventure of the universe.

To talk about God in terms of the experience of old people is to allow an understanding to emerge which goes beyond the rigid boundaries imposed by consumerist and exclusive societies. It is to try to overthrow the totalitarianisms of civil and religious societies. It is to open the doors to the construction of a theological pluralism in which not only races, cultures, sexes and social classes can express themselves, but also every age-group out of the wealth of its lived experience. To talk about God from the experience of old people is finally to open the doors lovingly to what will come to all of us, what will come and is an integral part of the human and cosmic process.

Conclusion

My discussion does not seek to draw conclusions. Aging as a moral issue is an open meditation. That meditation must continue, nourished by tears, by the daily labour of thousands of aging people, nourished also by the joy, by the little hopes, by acts of tenderness, by the search for more human ways of living.

There is little talking, thinking or writing about old age in Latin America.[2] Writing about the subject in theological anthropology is really scarce. It is a struggle which as yet has very few activists.

My aim in this short article has been to open up a few lines of enquiry which will need to be extended, broadened, reviewed and brought to a conclusion. The 'morality of aging', the 'theology of old age', are expressions of a fundamental human concern, reconciliation – of human nature with itself and the universe. This reconciliation, the delayed coming to birth of humanity, a process which seems never-ending, which even seems to begin again in each generation, feeds the hope of those who love the justice of the kingdom, who are passionately involved with human nature and the earth, and who always stubbornly hope anew for the victory of life in all its dimensions.

Translated by Francis McDonagh

Bibliography

Eclea Bosi, *Memoria e sociedade*, Biblioteca de letras e ciências humanas, série 1, Estudos brasileiros, Editora da Universidade de São Paulo, São Paulo 1987
Jean Maisondieu, *La crépuscule de la raison*, Paris 1989
P. Ariès, *L'enfant et la vie familiale sous l'ancien régime*, Paris 1960
id., *Essais sur l'histoire de la mort en occident*, Paris 1975

Notes

1. Simone de Beauvoir, *La Vieillesse* I, Paris 1970, pp. 17–18. The addition '(and women)' is mine. I am sure that Simone de Beauvoir would approve.

2. I should like to mention the important contribution made by Vemea ('Vejez en Mexico: Estudio y Acción', Apdo Postal 1912, Cuernavaca, Mexico), which is a pioneer study of the issues, and on ways of educating elderly people.

Ethics and Aging in Africa

Bénézet Bujo

As many investigations have shown, aging is one of the most disturbing questions in industrial society. An inter-cultural dialogue, above all with non-Western cultures, seems important for the solution of this problem. How old people are treated in these cultures, most of which have still not *totally* been encompassed by the modern Western mentality and are still faithful to their own tradition, is decidedly different from their treatment in European and American society. On the other hand, however, it must be remembered that, given modern technology and the modern economic system, the world is being brought increasingly close together, and at a hectic pace. This could bring violent changes to the old traditions of the non-Western world. So those who reflect on such traditions may not plead innocence over against Western society; they need to save their own culture and identity from a possible modern catastrophe.

With this in view, I shall approach the problem of aging in Africa here in three stages. First of all I shall describe the basic concept of African culture and religion. Only from this perspective is it possible to understand correctly attitudes towards older people. I shall then add some reflections of my own on the threat posed by modernity to the traditional approach.

I. What is the basis of respect for old people?

In the African world, everything can be derived from the basic concept of 'life'. The origin of life is God himself, who in Africa is not – as many Western scholars think – regarded as an impersonal monistic principle or a nameless source of energy. God stands 'over against' human beings.[1] Many divine names and prayers attest this irrefutably.[2]

The life that comes from God has a hierarchical order. Right at the top come the ancestors. Then follow the oldest members of the community, i.e. the fathers (and also the mothers) of families, the head of the whole family alliance and the chieftain or king. Depending on their function and task in the community, they form the link between the ancestors and the living, who only in this way can participate in fullness of life. However, it has to be pointed out here that this participation is never one-sided, nor only from above downwards. In the African context there is a reciprocal relationship between all members of the community. Nor is this community limited to its earthly members; it is two-dimensional and thus also embraces the dead of a tribe. All members of a family or tribe live in interdependence. They can influence one another positively or negatively. The good or evil that the individual does furthers or diminishes the life-power of the whole clan. It follows from this that the handing on of life in the comprehensive sense is the supreme commandment of African ethics. No one may keep life for themselves; they must allow other members of the family or clan to participate in it. Anyone who has behaved selfishly has sinned against God himself as the ground of life. The cult of ancestors can also be understood in terms of this basic concept. If the dead and those who remain behind form a single community, there is an interaction between them. Those who remain behind know that they depend on the dead and above all on the ancestors for the growth of life. On the other hand, the dead and the ancestors cannot live happily without support from the earthly community. Striving for life in abundance or anxiety at the diminution of the power of life are decisive for this two-dimensional relationship.

In this context the moral element also plays a decisive role. Great significance is attached to the words, commands and prohibitions of the ancestors and the elders of the community in so far as they document those experiences which have made possible community life to the present day. The fate of the individual, and indeed of all the living and dead of a clan, depends on these particular experiences. They may not simply be passed over and done away with in the name of modernity. Anyone who despises the ancestors and the elders and offends against the laws and precepts established by them chooses death instead of life. But this death will affect not only the individual but the whole community. For as a saying from Burundi puts it, if a member of a family has eaten dog meat, all the members of the clan are dishonoured as a result (*Umuryambwa aba uwe agatukisha umurvango*). Love and obligation to parents are also rooted specifically in this social solidarity. Placide Tempels is right in saying that the important principle in this respect is: 'The power of those older by birth always remains stronger than that of those born later and always exercises influence on it.'[3]

No wonder that, for example, children remain dependent on the life power of their parents to an advanced age. Although they may go their own way as they become mature and lead independent lives, this should not be understood in terms of Western individuality. While Western people know living beings 'in the form of individuals' and look with mistrust on the influence of the group or community as a threat to individual freedom, in Africa the problem for people is different. If – as I have already stressed – community is necessary for life, there can be no individual development outside this group which supports the individual. Individuals can attain freedom only in community with others, in 'communality'. In other words, one becomes human only in the wider family, and the totality, the wider family, is represented in the individual. 'One is "at home" only in one's father's house; one's own house is a division of one's father's house.'[4]

The same thing is true of the tribe. The individual finds identity only in common with other members of the clan community. All this explains why great importance is attached to love of parents in black African praxis. Blessing, good fortune and a harmonious life depend on whether one has shown parents and elders of the tribal community sincere love and esteem.[5]

It should be noted that the respect due is above all shown to one's parents and the elders of the tribal community. Nevertheless, respect is not limited to them, but affects all people and all those who – regardless of their origin – are older, and therefore can be called 'big brothers' or 'big sisters'. Anyone, even a stranger, who does not belong to my tribal community is still the 'property of the Other', namely God's creature; such people have their own dignity and deserve respect and love.

The concept of life sketched out here is indispensable for understanding African society in its concern for the old.

II. Aging as experiential wisdom and as a task

1. Towards a just treatment of the old

Generally speaking, aging in Africa is in no way a negative process. For example, in East Africa it is customary to use the term *mzee* (the old person), a Kiswahili word, for any adult of a particular age. Similarly, in Kiswahili parliament is called *baraza la wazee*, 'council of elders'. Being old or aging in this connection means 'becoming wiser'. So it is very important to treat old people well, not least because of their wisdom. Though biologically they can give no more life, they can still beget life through their experience and wisdom and hand it on to those who are younger. An apt proverb in Zaire is: 'The mouth of an old man has bad breath, but does not lie' (*Kinwa cha mzee kina harufu, likini hakina uwongo*). However, that does not mean that the old person always speaks truth as understood in a Western sense, but rather that his words prompt reflection and convey experiential wisdom. The growth of the life of both individual and community depends on these words. It is significant that some tribes in Africa compare the female sex organ with an old man. In the sexual act it 'eats' the man, receives the 'seed' and transforms it into life which is given anew. Similarly, the old man receives the word through the ear – an organ which is similar to the female sex organ – and transforms it into the wisdom which emerges from the mouth as life.[7]

The experience and wisdom spoken of in the African context show some parallels with the Old Testament in respect of the fourth commandment. As in the Old Covenant, so here, the prosperity of children in having possessions and other necessary things in life depends on whether they are ready to hearken to the wisdom of parents and elders and make use of their experience. Parents and the elders of the community know better how life comes into being and how to preserve it, defend it and hand it on. So it is not permissible to cast out parents and elders, even if they are old in years – indeed, precisely then. This would be an offence against the supreme good, namely life, which is ultimately founded in God himself. Here it should be stressed that even when old people's constitutions are such that they cannot enrich society either by wisdom or by any other contribution, it is an unavoidable task to continue to give them life by respecting their dignity and their status in respect of the ancestors, to whom they are drawing close.

This supreme status of the old is made clear to children from their youngest days. They are taught from the beginning how to treat the solitary, the sick, the weak and particularly the old. They are asked to help an old man in the fields, to cook or draw water for him. They are brought up to provide company for an old neighbour, to stay overnight with her, so that she does not feel lonely, to get firewood for her, and so on. It should be noted that, as in the Old Testament, duty towards parents and the old is not primarily a command for small children. It is more the task of adults to look after parents and old people. But they are familiarized with this care even as children. On the other hand, these same children are prepared for aging. Anyone who is to merit the title 'wise' must first practise those virtues which mark out an experienced elder. Even in sickness, suffering and death they must try to preserve an attitude which offers a lesson in wisdom to others. So it is not unusual for an old woman or an old man to gather all the members of their family and their friends around them as they die, to give them a blessing and to entrust to them last words of wisdom as a testimony.

However, for someone to remain brave even when dying is part of a process of growth which lasts a whole lifetime. In the African tradition children had to learn this not least in initiation rites, the aim of which was among other things to teach young men bravery and to live as examples for others. All this is to be given particular expression in old age.

But an old person who wants to hand on personal wisdom and experience is in no way striving for power. For example, on the basis of his wisdom an aged father must recognize the right time to entrust everything to his son, so that the son may still benefit from the counsels of his father. Withdrawal from public life here does not mean passivity and a refusal to play an active part in social life. People retire in order to be able to initiate others better. To put it even more clearly, the predecessor, the *mzee* (the elder), is not deprived of power, nor does the successor emerge as victor, but as one who wants to gain a better knowledge about handing on life, so that he can be a true link between the ancestors and the earthly community of which he is head.

I shall now discuss briefly this relationship with the ancestors, which is the basis of the authority of the elders and leaders of the community.

2. The significance of anamnetic thought in Africa

To understand the treatment of the old more profoundly we need to recall African solidarity with the ancestors. This solidarity not only relates to the 'defeated' of history (to use Walter Benjamin's term) but seeks to preserve the memory of all those who made the present day livable for those who remain behind and who opened up the future to them.[8] This is an anamnetic solidarity through which descendants prove their identity, an identity which can be rightly understood only in the light of the history of their forebears. In other words, the present-day generation lives on what its predecessors have sown. Anyone who reaps today must keep this constantly in mind. The idea of forebears as benefactors is therefore a fundamental part of ancestor worship, which concerns not only life still to be conceived but also life that is already conceived. We can call what is stressed here *gratitude*. This in turn does not relate exclusively to the invisible community of those who are already dead, but also extends to those who are still alive on earth, especially the oldest among them. The latter are drawn into the anamnetic solidarity because they, too, have helped to shape the history in which the younger ones are to continue to work. This proximity of old people to the ancestors means that they may not be driven into solitude but must be taken up in to the solidarity of the tribe. Their presence among those living on earth has a sacramental significance. For they make the ancestors present, and in a decisive way ensure the handing on of life through the tradition of the wisdom of the ancestors. So it is to them that the members of the tribe owe the foundation of their existence, and what was begun by the older generation opens the eyes of the younger ones afresh to some values.

I repeat the point: because of anamnetic gratitude and solidarity it is an enormous evil, indeed a sin which cries out to heaven, to deny the old human dignity and make them disposable people. But anyone who is concerned to avert this evil must treat old people in such a way as to rid them of the feeling of 'uselessness'. As long as they are able, we are to include them in the communications of society by giving them, too, the right to take part in our discourse, so that we carry on *together* the society which for the most part was built up by them. From an African perspective it would be not only exploitation, but even murder to delete the old people from our memory and not allow them to go on living near us and our families. Those who forget the old also forget the history that preceded them and which put at their disposal all by which they live today. This would be to act like a Melchizedek, without father and mother. Again from the African perspective, it is neither responsible nor right to build oneself a kind of paradise and make for oneself a more or less fine life while allowing to fall into forgetfulness the figures of history, the old, who often had to work hard and suffer severe deprivations so that their children could have a better life than they did. Was all this just a natural duty, for which no one any longer owes any thanks?

III. Final considerations

Given the complex problem which I addressed at the beginning, that above all in the West we are being confronted with an increasing number of old people, it is urgent to find a solution which has human dignity. A look at African culture makes the limitations of a purely technological civilization even clearer. For example no old people's home, however comfortable, can ever replace human proximity and warmth.

Precisely in this connection Africa has the task of reflecting once again on its cultural heritage. We cannot dismiss the possibility that modernity can destroy the good in tradition, or indeed has already partly dispelled it.

As far as aging is concerned, the following points are worth thinking about. Though aging is still regarded as valuable – because it brings wisdom – in the post-colonial period there is a danger that it will be distorted and devalued. So today it is even more indispensable than ever to keep in view the virtue which must mark out old age as wisdom. I already observed above that wisdom can no longer be identified with a wisdom which is carefully defined in philosophical terms. It consists primarily in silence and listening. Only those who can be silent, listen, and assimilate what has been heard by meditation in the depths of their being, as in a womb, are in a position to beget and bear wisdom. They will then also enable other people to continue boldly along the way of life.

That wisdom understood in this way is nowadays threatened in many respects can no longer be denied. Purely intellectual wisdom is so over-valued by schools, universities and literacy campaigns that the wisdom of old age is being lost. Omniscient intellectuals think that they need no longer listen to the old. They have no silence nor capacity to listen, and if they reach advanced old age, they will have no wisdom to hand on to the younger ones.

The same is true of the exercise of power in present-day Africa. Those who hold power are no longer links between the ancestors and the people and are not primarily concerned with handing on life, but with prestige, money and riches. Even their own clan community – in contrast to traditional practice – may participate only as long as they do not produce any opposition. Moreover the council of elders, which had the task of correcting the chief and on occasion deposing him in the name of the ancestors, is lacking. Apart from this institutionalized council of elders, there was also a non-institutionalized council in which the elders mutually encouraged and corrected one another. They could also quite informally take the initiative in pillorying evil in society. All this meant that the old had to provide a good example.

Aging in Africa today could lead to similar problems to those in Europe, unless a stop is put to the distortion of tradition. Those who are growing old today, who are pulled to and fro between pure knowledge, power and riches, have not lived in a way which can provide an example of wisdom to the younger ones, and they can be mocked and rejected by these as inexperienced, neo-colonial elders (*mzee kijana*).[9] The bow is not yet over-stretched, but it is important to take preventive measures in time before it is too late. Here church theology and state have to work hand in hand.

Translated by John Bowden

Notes

1. J. M. Ela, *Ma foi d'Africain*, Paris 1985.
2. For what follows see also B. Bujo, *Afrikanische Theologie in ihrem gesellschaft-lichen Kontext*, Düsseldorf 1986, 21ff.; id., 'Verantwortung und Solidarität. Christliche Ethik in Afrika', *Stimmen der Zeit* 109, 1984, 795–804.
3. P. Tempels, *Bantu-Philosophie. Ontologie und Ethik*, Heidelberg 1956, 33; id., *La philosophie bantoue*, Elizabethville 1945.
4. T. Sündermeier, *Nur gemeinsam können wir leben. Der Menschenbild schwarz-afrikanischer Religionen*, Gütersloh ²1990, 26.
5. Bujo, *Afrikanische Theologie* (n. 2), 39.

6. Ibid.

7. For the significance of 'word' in the African context cf. M. Griaule, *Schwarze Genesis. Ein afrikanischer Schöpfungsbericht*, Freiburg im Breisgau 1970. Cf. also Sündermeier, *Nur gemeinsam* (n. 4), 30ff.

8. For more detail see B. Bujo, 'Gibt es eine spezifisch afrikanische Ethik? Eine Anfrage an westliches Denken', *Stimmen der Zeit* 114, 1989, 591–601: 595–7.

9. This Kiswahili expression literally means 'young elder' and may stress lack of experience and qualification. At the same time the person concerned is denied the title 'elder'.

Creative Social Responses to Aging

Public Policy Options for Family Caregiving

Drew Christiansen

Family caregiving is the oldest form of assistance to impaired and chronically ill elderly. After decades of government expansion of nursing homes and other services for infirm old people, policymakers are beginning to turn again to families as the primary caretakers of the elderly. After examining the sociological forces which have both renewed interest in inter-generational caregiving and posed questions about its long-term viability, this article elaborates an ethical rationale for family caregiving, responds to the objection that family caregiving is paternalistic, and reviews some model programmes for assisting familial caregivers.

Sociological background: an intersection of problems

Several sociological trends converge to set the parameters for future care of the elderly. To begin with, there is an absolute and relative growth in the numbers of old people. In the United States, for example, in 1900 the elderly (aged sixty-five and older) numbered 3.1 million and were 4.1% of the population; by 1984 they numbered 28 million and accounted for 11.9% of the population. While the elderly population has been swelling in numbers, the size of the younger population has diminished, leaving fewer children to look after aged parents and generating a narrowed tax base from which to garner revenue for public support of the aged. Moreover, the numbers of the very old are growing even faster than those of the aged population as a whole. Men and women over eighty-five are the fastest-growing subgroup among the aged; they now count for 1% of the US population and by 2050 should rise to 5% of the total.

The greater life expectancy of old people places new burdens on adult children who themselves may suffer disabilities associated with early and middle old age. The burdens of care are complicated still further by the greater incidence of chronic illness among elderly survivors. Greater life-expectancy for the very old is associated with increased disease and disability, thereby imposing heavier demands on caregivers for longer periods of time. The average caregiver (a woman) is now expected to spend eighteen years raising her children and nineteen years caring for her parents. At the same time, as a result of changes in public priorities, more and more family members have become directly involved in caregiving. According to one study, family caregiving in the US has increased by 38% in the last decade.

This increase in family caregiving appears counter-intuitive, in that simultaneously with the rise in the demand for family caregiving, changing family styles and other sociological trends raise questions about whether family bonds will be strong enough over the medium-term future to preserve the family unit as the principal source of care to frail and impaired old people.

In the first place, the augmentation of women in the work-force has reduced the available pool of full-time caregivers. It has also placed still greater strains on middle-aged women already burdened by homemaking chores and assistance to teenage and young adult children as well as job responsibilities. Publicly supported programmes which provide 'assistance with daily living' delay the time when elders are forced to be dependent on family members, but they also insure that inter-generational caregiving begins at a point where the demands on family members will be more serious.

Secondly, the dispersal of family members over wide distances has meant, at least for some segments of the population, that caregiving is an intermittent undertaking or must be conducted with the help of semi-skilled intermediaries or professional service agencies. While forecasters predicted that the movement of retirees to age-segregated communities and to more hospitable climates, like the US Sunbelt, would also be a barrier to inter-generational commitment, reverse migrations of the aged to their former neighbourhoods and to the homes of adult children seem to re-establish family ties at the elders' time of greatest need.

Thirdly, we have yet to see what the impact of divorce, single-parent families and changing family styles will be on eldercare. While social scientists anticipate a decline in inter-generational commitment, so far they can only report some weakening of 'expressed' commitments. But expressions of anticipated commitment have always been far lower than actual behaviour, and current behaviour indicates even greater participation by family members than that found in the post-World War II period. Thus, though stresses on the inter-generational family have grown dramatically, there is no hard evidence to date that they have put family care to the elderly in jeopardy.

Demographic pressures on family caregivers have been aggravated by public policy decisions. Since the late 1970s the perception of 'inter-generational inequity', prompted by the improved welfare of the elderly at a time when other (younger) sectors of the society enjoy smaller benefits from public spending, has resulted in the US and Scandinavia in reduced willingness on the part of the general public to pay for programmes for the elderly. In the US and Britain, cuts in government services have made it more difficult to meet some needs of infirm elderly people. In the US, restrictions on Medicare have resulted in a limited privatization of health care delivery in which certain forms of medical treatment and long-term care become out of reach of the poor and the middle class. Much of the increase in family caregiving in the US seems to have resulted from the statistical management of hospital cases, imposed by government regulators, which led to premature release of aged patients.

One proposal by the distinguished American ethicist Daniel Callahan for allocating scarce medical resources in the future is to restrict the treatment available to the elderly at public expense to chronic and palliative care. Another option would be to apply a needs test to publicly supported health care, forcing affluent older people to pay for medical treatment, so that old age would no longer be grounds for entitlement.

The positive side of debates over rationing care of the elderly has been a shift of interest away from acute medical treatment to care as such, and from medical institutions to families as a focus of policy-making. Callahan and others defend this shift, arguing that what elderly people need most is caring, and that the costly application of intensive medical resources results only in extending the suffering of the very old. While in the past welfare-state approaches to care of the elderly have been concerned largely with direct provision of service to elderly clients, the convergence of several lines of social pressure has resulted in experimentation with new modes of care, such as adult day health care and respite care, which provide family members with needed assistance and relief from their caregiving responsibilities. Others include support groups for caregivers, caregiver counselling services, and hospices for the terminally ill. These new developments are most promising because they lend support to the caregiving system which not only does the lion's share of direct care, but, as I shall try to show, is also the most appropriate means of caring for the elderly.

To sum up, while sociological trends seem to indicate reasons for anticipating the weakening of inter-generational ties, actual behaviour, abetted by constriction of some forms of government support of the elderly, demonstrates greater involvement on the part of family members in care of the elderly than at any time since the Second World War.

The needs of the elderly and the shape of care for them

Family care is the traditional approach to caregiving for the aged. In the biblical religions, the fourth commandment – 'Honour your father and your mother' – enjoined adult children to support their parents in old age and to preserve them from disgrace when they were affected by frailty or senility. The degree of family involvement with elderly relatives differs from culture to culture. For some years, however, sociological mythmaking by self-proclaimed 'modernizers' promoting individualism and the so-called 'nuclear family' tended to obscure the degree to which the traditional value of care of the elderly continued to be honoured in contemporary Western societies. In the United States, for example, social gerontologists have shown that for more than thirty years (1945–1980) family members cared for two-thirds of the country's infirm elderly. Despite adverse pressures which we have discussed, which continue to lead social scientists to predict a decline of family participation in caregiving, the level of family involvement climbed to 80% between 1980 and 1985. By one estimate, 'informal networks' now provide as much as 90% of the care for infirm and chronically-ill elderly in the US.

While the increase in the incidence in family caregiving has still to be explained and offers some reason for concern, in that some relatives who might not have shouldered this responsibility at other times now apparently feel pressure to do so, the growing recognition of the contribution families make to care of the elderly and the recent interest in family caregiving as an alternative to exorbitant public spending for the elderly presents an opportunity to reflect anew on the suitability of family care to the special needs of aged men and women.

Dignity in aging: the moral rationality of familial dependence

Impaired and chronically-ill old people have several needs: (a) support in daily living, (b) personal care, (c) companionship and (d) autonomy with respect to major life-decisions. *Support* refers to assistance in activities that are a routine part of living: shopping, cooking, cleaning, banking, and so on. *Care* consists essentially in nursing chores, such as bathing, grooming and supervising medication. *Companionship* involves sharing social activities such as visiting, listening to stories, sharing feelings, and so on. *Autonomy* refers to the authority competent adults exercise over the fundamental aspects of their lives. In the case of frail elderly, these would include living circumstances, health care, terminal treatment. In infirm old age, interest in autonomy over the complete range of life choices is reduced with respect to need for support, care and companionship. In so far as families provide these goods for aged relatives, they are contributing to the dignity of those elderly loved ones.

As their infirmity and disability grow, elderly people need to rely on others to supply things they once provided for themselves. For most, this social dependency is preferable to the major alternatives: isolated living and institutionalization. While public programmes make it possible for aged persons to live independently for longer periods than earlier generations, isolated living usually aggravates the hardships of aging because those who are isolated must increasingly forego activities by which they supported themselves in everyday life. Inevitably, curtailing such activities results in deprivation and hardship. Statistically, isolated elderly people are the most afflicted in their age group. They suffer the most disease, they tend to be mentally confused, and they live in the most degraded surroundings. Accordingly, faced with such a prospect, it is reasonable for impaired or ill old people to choose to rely on family members rather than to endure worsening conditions on their own.

Institutionalization, while it provides especially for the medical and nursing needs of the elderly person, also has many drawbacks. Ordinarily, elderly people regard institutionalization as a last resort. Nursing home patients tend to be overwhelmingly 'familyless' persons without close relatives to care for them, or very old people whose children are themselves too impaired by age to look after them. While they show great reluctance in burdening adult children and other family members prematurely and prefer to live independently as long as they can, when they are impaired old men and women prefer family care to placement in long-term care facilities. Significantly, they are reconciled to institutional care only after family members have arrived at the limits of their abilities to care for them.

It is easy to see why institutionalization is a less desirable alternative. While some few elderly people may prefer it as a way to remain independent of relatives, for most it requires an even greater surrender of personal freedom than familial caregiving arrangements. In the institution, the elderly person must accommodate to a greater degree to routines not of her or his own choosing. Care will also be less personal. Staff do not often have the occasion to build up long-term relationships with patients; and they must distribute their time over many patients. Because long-term care patients frequently require much attention to physical needs, staff have little occasion to spend social time with them. Even quality nursing care will tend to be less personal, indulging the patient's likes and dislikes very little. To this, one need only add the stigma which perceives institutionalization as a kind of 'abandonment' – a prejudice not borne out by the facts of family loyalty to long-term care patients – to see why elderly people once more prefer family care to institutional caregiving arrangements.

For some years ethicists worried about the potential for paternalism latent in familial dependence of the elderly, and social critics and investigative reporters pontificated about the dangers of abuse and exploitaiton of them. The ethicists, as it turned out, based their critique on an inordinate estimate of the value of freedom in personal life. That appraisal proved especially inappropriate for the frail and impaired elderly, in that their demand for freedom from others was outweighed by their need of support and care to sustain their physical well-being and for companionship to strengthen their spirits. The excessive emphasis Anglo-American, as well as German, bioethics placed on the individual was misplaced at any stage of life, but it was particularly inappropriate for enfeebled elderly people and their family members. As the gerontologist Margaret Blenkner has shown, dependency is a normal development for late-life families. For the elderly person, it represents a rational preference for welfare and companionship over abstract freedom, and for family members it counts as an effort to relieve the discomforts of old age for a loved one, and in so doing to sustain the elderly person's dignity despite physical loss and mental decline.

The moral rationale for family care, therefore, lies in the complexity of the values which compose human dignity. Contrary to the liberal view that human dignity consists exclusively in the exercise of individual freedom, the worth of the person is displayed in a variety of ways including physical care and social cultivation. In advanced old age, when impairment and illness threaten the capacity for independent living, family care is preferable to other arrangements because it best satisfies the set of basic values which constitute human dignity. In the family setting, old people find physical support and care, social interaction, and a wider margin of effective freedom than elsewhere.

Intergenerational friendship: a neglected need

The intimacy of the family setting is one of the reasons why elderly people choose family care over institutionalization and programmes of assistance in everyday living. Ironically, one of the areas in which elderly people express the most dissatisfaction is the quantity and quality of social time they spend with children and other family members. The family's failure in this regard can be explained by the temporal, psychic and physical demands of caregiving, by the varieties of roles discharged by the primary caregiver, and by the difficulties both generations experience in role reversal. All the same, *companionship* remains a need of the impaired elderly person which families could satisfy better than they have. The loss of agemates by death, impairment or immobility means that elderly people have very few intimates with whom they can share their experience at a time when they are undergoing dramatic and disorienting changes in their lives. Accordingly, for the most part family caregivers and other household members constitute the social world of housebound and bedfast elders. If they are going to deal with the grievous changes which are taking place in their lives, they must do so in the bosom of the family.

Three spiritual tasks face the frail elderly. First, they must *integrate their lives*. Psychologists tell us that this is the function of the often repetitive storytelling old men and women rehearse. These narratives help old people to find meaning and significance in the events of their lives and serve to reconcile them with their finitude. By listening to these stories, asking questions, and showing their interest and appreciation, family members assist the elderly in 'life-review'.

Secondly, old people must *face up to loss and diminishment*. Accepting loss is difficult at any time of life, but in old age it is especially hard. Most of life, people can compensate for losses. But even with today's medical advances and technological conveniences, there comes a time when old people can no longer compensate for their deficits. In addition, old age is a time of multiple losses. Physical decrements accumulate, disabilities grow, limitations multiply, and more and more friends and relatives die. So in late old age there is much grieving to do, and there are few people to mourn with. By hearing their complaints, by calming their fears, and comforting them with their presence, family members assist the elderly in meeting the succession of losses which can so easily dispirit them.

Some of the losses of advanced age, moreover, undermine elderly people's sense of themselves as persons. Loss of mobility, lack of control over bodily functions, the inability to speak, loss of memory: all these deprivations subvert people's sense of themselves as agents who exercise control over themselves and the world around them. The inward experience of diminishment requires reassurance of one's lasting worth which comes most naturally from those loved ones who have shared one's life.

Finally, the very old must *meet the ultimate challenge of death*. While this encounter is necessarily one a person must carry out alone, the presence and prayerful concern of family members can ease fears and assist, even enhance, dying as a human event and an act of faith in divine grace for the aged.

Family members are usually unprepared to meet these spiritual tasks of companionship to the elderly. It is difficult for many to talk about ultimate things. Many have not themselves pondered the significance of finitude, diminishment and death in their own lives. Yet, unless primary caregivers are willing to discuss such issues, elderly people will have no one with whom to share their final passage. Accordingly, the church, in the person of clergy, pastoral counsellors and spiritual directors, bears a responsibility to teach caregivers and their families how to discuss the existential mysteries of aging and dying with the aged and how generally to minister to them in their passage.

Family care and public policy

The potential for spiritual friendship between generations of one family is one of several reasons supporting the family as the natural home of care of the elderly. Other reasons include, as we have seen, the undesirability of the alternatives, the ability of family members to adjust to providing shifting levels of support and care, the intimacy involved in care of the ill and disabled, and the shared history possessed by families. In addition, even where a great variety of programmes are available for independent care of the elderly, family members supply most of the care for infirm and chronically ill old people. Given the stresses on the contemporary family, it makes sense, therefore, to look to public support for caregiving families as one significant way in which government can assist old people and relieve the excessive burden felt by today's family caregivers.

In recent years, there have been a number of creative initiatives for assisting families in meeting their caregiving responsibilities. Three of these are adult day health care, respite services, and hospices for the dying.

While some European countries and Canada make direct payments to families who care for dependent older relatives, caregivers appear to prefer the provision of services to monetary compensation. Primary forms of assistance are preferred either because they offer some benefit the family is unable to provide itself, such as physical therapy or skilled nursing care, or because they afford relief from the continuous burden of care. Adult day health care provides both sorts of benefits, offering skilled assistance for the elderly at the same time as it gives relief to the caregiver. Respite care, while it can include skilled care, aims primarily at allowing caregivers time to recover from illness, meet other family needs, or simply to rest from their labours. Finally, hospices provide specialized physical and spiritual care for the dying and their families. Public policies which would support such services to families provide the best hope for the future of long-term care of the elderly.

Another major need of family caregivers, which could be provided by private voluntary organizations like hospitals and educational institutions as well as by governments, is education for family caregivers. For caregivers need to know how to distinguish normal aging from graver disorders. They ought to be able to anticipate major transitions in an old person's condition, and know how to respond to those changes and where they can acquire specialized assistance. They also need to foresee the strains they and their families will feel and to be informed about resources for dealing with those pressures. A public policy which aims at maximizing care for infirm old people would make a wise investment in family and caregiver education.

For Further Reading

Carmen Barros, 'Catholicism, Lifestyles, and the Wellbeing of the Elderly', *Journal of Religion and Aging* 4 (3/4), Summer/Fall 1988, 109–18

Daniel Callahan, *Setting Limits: Medical Goals in an Aging Society*, New York 1987

James F. Childress, 'Ensuring Care, Respect, and Fairness for the Elderly', *Hastings Center Report*, October 1984, 27–31

Drew Christiansen, *When My Strength Is Spent: A Theological Ethics of Caregiving to the Elderly* (forthcoming)

Raymond Collins, 'The Fourth Commandment: For Children or Adults', in *Christian Morality: Biblical Foundations*, Notre Dame, IN: 1986, 82–100

Charles E. Curran, 'Filial Responsibility for an Elderly Parent', *Social Thought* 11 (2), Summer 1985, 40–52

Generations, Fall 1985 (this issue of the journal is devoted entirely to informal caregiving)

J. Gordon Harris, *Biblical Perspectives on Aging: God and the Elderly*, Philadelphia 1987

Nancy R. Hooyman and Wendy Lastbader, *Taking Care: Supporting Older People and Their Families*, New York 1986

Rosalie A. Kane, 'A Family Caregiving Policy: Should We Have One?', *Generations*, Fall 1985, 33–6

Marcia G. Ory, 'The Burden of Care: A Familial Perspective', *Generations*, Fall 1985, 14–18

Mark Siegler, 'Should Age Be a Criterion in Health Care?', *Hastings Center Report*, October 1984, 24–7

Robert M. Veatch, 'Autonomy's Temporary Triumph', *Hastings Center Report*, October 1984, 38–40

Alan Wolfe, *Whose Keeper? Social Science and Moral Obligation*, Berkeley 1989

Contributors

Rosa Fernández Herranz is Spanish, a mother of three, with a medical and surgical doctorate from the University of Valladolid (1975), specializing in neurology. She practised medicine in a Catholic hospital in Zaire from 1968 to 1970, and has since worked in the neurology department of the University Hospital in Valladolid, where she is at present head clinician. Her preference has long been for psycho-geriatrics, particularly the study and treatment of Alzheimer's disease. She has lectured widely and published several articles on psycho-geriatrics, neurological subjects and medical ethics.

Gerardo Hernández Rodríguez holds a doctorate in politics and sociology from the University of Alcalà-Madrid, and a diploma in political sociology from the Spanish Institute of Political Studies. He lectures on the sociology of the family at the Pontifical University of Comillas-Madrid. He has written several studies on the sociology of the family, education and demography, including a series on the 'Health Demography' of adolescence, adulthood and old age, published by the Ministry of Health. His doctoral thesis dealt with the subject, 'Abortion of Spain: Analysis of a socio-political process'.

Elisabeth von der Lieth was born in Kulm, Czechoslovakia in 1918. After leaving school she studied German, French and history, and between 1941 and 1965 was a secondary school teacher. From 1965 to 1968 she was head of a study seminar for training secondary school teachers. She has written articles in various journals (including *Stimmen der Zeit*) on the theory and politics of education and numerous book reviews. She lectures on anthropological questions in institutes of adult education.

Daniel Callahan is co-founder and Director of The Hastings Center. He has a BA from Yale and a PhD from Harvard. He is an elected member of the Institute of Medicine, National Academy of Sciences, USA. He is the author or editor of thirty books. The most recent include *What Kind of Life: The Limits of Medical Progress* (1990), and *Setting Limits: Medical Goals in An Aging Society* (1987).

ROBERT MARTIN-ACHARD is a pastor. He studied at Geneva, Basle and Zurich and has taught in Montpellier, Kinshasa and Antananarivo. He is an honorary professor of the universities of Geneva and Neuchâtel. He is the author of a number of books and articles on the Old Testament, including *Permanence de l'Ancien Testament. Recherches d'exégèse et de théologie*, Cahiers de la Revue de Théologie et de Philosophie 11, Geneva, Lausanne and Neuchâtel 1984.

HELEN OPPENHEIMER was born in London in 1926; she studied at Oxford, where she also took the degree of B.Phil. in philosophy in 1952. She is married to Sir Michael Oppenheimer, Bt. She taught ethics at Cuddesdon Theological College from 1964 to 1969, and has served on several Church of England commissions on marriage and marriage discipline, and on the Inter-Anglican Theological and Doctrinal Commission. Publications include: *Law and Love* (1962); *The Character of Christian Morality* (1965, ²1974); *Incarnation and Immanence* (1973); *The Hope of Happiness* (1983); *Looking Before and After* (The Archbishop of Canterbury's Lent Book for 1988, published in USA as *The Hope of Heaven*); *Marriage* (1990); and articles in books and periodicals including *Concilium* (1973), *A New Dictionary of Christian Ethics* (1986), and *Doctors' Decisions*, ed. Dunstan & Shinebourne (1989).

PAUL SCHOTSMANS was born in Bekkevoort, Belgium in 1950. A priest, he studied pedagogical sciences and theology and gained his doctorate at the Catholic University of Louvain with a thesis on 'The Theory of Values as a Sign of a Secularized Society?'. He teaches medical ethics in the Faculty of Medicine there, and since 1986 he has at the same time been Director of the Centre for Biomedical Ethics at the Catholic University of Louvain.

WALTER J. BURGHARDT SJ is co-editor of the series *Ancient Christian Writers* and Senior Fellow of the Woodstock Theological Center, a research institute examining moral values and the problems facing contemporary society. Former editor-in-chief of *Theological Studies*, he has specialized in patristic theology and in preaching. He has written twelve books, among them *The Image of God in Man according to Cyril of*

Alexandria and *Preaching: The Art and the Craft*. Former president of the Catholic Theological Society of America and the American Theological Society, he has received sixteen honorary degrees from American colleges and universities. He has served on the International Papal Theological Commission, the Faith and Order Commission of the World Council of Churches, and the US Lutheran-Roman Catholic Dialogue.

EUGENE C. BIANCHI, a Professor of Religion at Emory University in Atlanta, Georgia, USA, specializes in humanistic studies that relate religion, psychology and culture. He has written two books on aging from psychospiritual perspectives: *Aging as a Spiritual Journey* and *On Growing Older*. He has also written a chapter in *Affirmative Aging* about confronting one's own death as an enhancement of life. In addition to publishing articles on aging, he has given many talks and conducted workshops on creative aging. He is at present doing research for a book of in-depth biographical interviews with older people who have been able to age in ways that give insight and encouragement to others.

MARTINA BLASBERG-KUHNKE was born in Hagen, Westphalia in 1958. She studied theology and educational science, gaining her doctorate. Married, between 1981 and 1987 she was academic assistant at the Seminar for Pastoral Theology and Religious Education in the University of Münster. Since then she has taught practical theology in the university and is studying for her Habilitation in religious education. Her publications include *Gerontologie und Praktische Theologie*, Düsseldorf 1985; (with Norbert Mette), *Kirche auf dem Weg ins Jahr 2000*, Düsseldorf 1986; and various contributions on community theology, pastoral work with the old, women's issues and adult education.

MARY JOHN MANANZAN OSB is the National Chairperson of *Gabriela*, a national federation of women's organizations. She is also the Dean of the College of St Scholastica's College and Director of the Institute of Women's Studies. She is co-foundress of the Citizen's Alliance for Consumer Protection of which she is the present Secretary General, and the Center for Women's Resources, of which she is the present Chairperson of the Board of Advisers.

IVONE GEBARA was professor of philosophy and theology at the theological institute of Recife (ITER), which was closed in December 1989. She is a member of the DEPA team, an interdisciplinary organization in Recife for the training of pastoral workers for poor communities. She is also a member of CESEP, an ecumenical organization in São Paulo devoted to popular education. She is a member of the Congregation of the Sisters of Notre Dame. She has published articles in international and Brazilian theological journals. Her books include *A Mulher faz teologia*, Petrópolis, RJ 1986; (with M. Clara Bingemer) *Mary, Mother of God, Mother of the Poor*, New York and London 1989; *As Incômodas filhas de Eva na Igreja da América Latina*, São Paulo 1989; *Levanta-te e anda*, São Paulo 1989.

BÉNÉZET BUJO was born in Drodro/Bunai, Zaire, in 1940. He studied philosophy and theology at the seminaries of Niangara and Murhesa, at the Lovanium University, Kinshasa, the University of Würzburg (where he gained his doctorate and teaching qualifications), and the Grabmann Institute in Munich. Between 1978 and 1989 he was Professor of Moral Theology in the Catholic Theological Faculty at Kinshasa; since 1989 he has been Ordinarius Professor of Moral Theology in the University of Freiburg, Switzerland. His publications include *Moral africaine et foi chrétienne*, Kinshasa 1976, ²1980; *Moralautonomie und Normenfindung bei Thomas von Aquin*, Paderborn and Munich 1979; *Les dix commandements pour quoi faire? Actualité du Problème en Afrique*, Kinshasa 1980, ²1985 (translated into English and Kiswahili); *Die Begründung des Sittlichen. Zur Frage des Eudämonismus bei Thomas von Aquin*, Paderborn and Munich 1984; *Afrikanische Theologie in ihrem gesellschaftlichen Kontext*, Düsseldorf 1986; *Le diaire d'un théologien africain*, Kinshasa 1987; *African Christian Morality at the Age of Inculturation*, Nairobi 1990.

DREW CHRISTIANSEN SJ is Bannan Scholar at Santa Clara University, California. He was formerly Associate Professor of Theology at the University of Notre Dame, Indiana, and taught at the Jesuit School of Theology at Berkeley, where he was director of the Graduate Theological Union's Center for Ethics and Social Policy. His book *When My Strength Is Spent: A Theological Ethics of Caregiving to the Elderly* will be published soon. He has written extensively on geriatric ethics. His essays on the topic have appeared in journals, including *Hastings Center Report*, *Journal of Humanistic Psychology* and *America*. His reference articles may be found in the *Encyclopedia of Bioethics*, the *New [US Westminster] Dictionary of Christian Ethics*, and the *New Dictionary of Catholic Social Thought*.

Members of the Advisory Committee for Moral Theology

Directors:

Lisa Sowle Cahill	Chestnut Hill/MA	USA
Dietmar Mieth	Neustetten	West Germany

Members:

Franz Böckle	Bonn-Röttgen	West Germany
Klaus Demmer	Rome	Italy
Margaret Farley	New Haven, Conn.	USA
Erich Fuchs	Lausanne/Geneva	Switzerland
Josef Fuchs SJ	Rome	Italy
Gerard Gilleman SJ	Barrackpore	India
Tullo Goffi	Brescia	Italy
Léonce Hamelin OFM	Montreal/Quebec	Canada
Bernard Häring CSSR	Gars am Inn	West Germany
Benedicta Hintersberger	Augsburg	West Germany
Antonio Hortelano	Rome/Madrid	Italy/Spain
Helmut Juros	Warsaw	Poland
Walter Kerber SJ	Munich	West Germany
Harry Kuitert	Amstelveen	The Netherlands
Richard McCormick SJ	Washington, DC	USA
Enda McDonagh	Maynooth	Ireland
Helen Oppenheimer	Jersey	Channel Islands
Bernard Quelquejeu OP	Paris	France
Warren Reich	Washington, DC	USA
René Simon	Paris	France
Jaime Snoek CSSR	Juiz de Fora, MG	Brazil
José Solozábal	Bilbao	Spain
Paul Sporken	Maastricht	The Netherlands
Xavier Thévenot	Paris	France
Marciano Vidal	Madrid	Spain

Back issues still available

1990 issues:

Other back numbers are available as follows: